How *Did* Sh...
MARKETING
SUCCESS

Women Lawyers Show You How to Move Beyond Tips to Implementation

EDITED BY
DEE A. SCHIAVELLI AND
AFI S. JOHNSON-PARRIS

ABALAW
PRACTICE
DIVISION
The Business of Practicing Law

Printed in the United States of America.

19 18 17 16 15   5 4 3 2 1

Library of Congress Cataloging-in-Publication Data

Marketing success, how did she do that? : women lawyers show you how to move beyond tips to implementation / edited by Afi S. Johnson-Parris and Dee A. Schiavelli. — First edition.
    pages cm
    Includes bibliographical references.
    ISBN 978-1-63425-133-4 (print : alk. paper)
    1. Women lawyers—United States—Marketing. 2. Women lawyers—United States—Handbooks, manuals, etc. I. Johnson-Parris, Afi S., editor. II. Schiavelli, Dee A. editor. III. American Bar Association. Law Practice Division, sponsoring body.
    KF316.5.M379 2015
    340'.0688—dc23

                                                                    2015011050

Discounts are available for books ordered in bulk. Special consideration is given to state bars, CLE programs, and other bar-related organizations. Inquire at Book Publishing, ABA Publishing, American Bar Association, 321 North Clark Street, Chicago, Illinois 60654-7598.

www.ShopABA.org

This book is dedicated to women lawyers everywhere who balance so many aspects of their personal and professional lives and still manage to grow their practices.

Contents

About the Authors

Many women have contributed to writing this book. Without their expertise, time, and energy, it could not have been done. Their backgrounds are diverse: some are attorneys, others are marketing experts in law firms, and others are marketing consultants with many years of working with lawyers. All are part of the ABA Women Rainmakers Committee. Here is a little about them, in alphabetical order:

Anne Collier, consultant
Arudia
www.arudia.com
(202) 449-9751 | anne@arudia.com
Anne Collier is a catalyst for lawyers and executives stepping into power. Her coaching and workshops on business development, branding, leadership, and communication help her clients create successful, fulfilling careers and get great results.

Beth Cuzzone, director of client service and business development
Goulston & Storrs, PC
www.goulstonstorrs.com
(617) 574-6525 | bcuzzone@goulstonstorrs.com
Beth Cuzzone is a founding member of the Legal Sales and Service Organization (legalsales.org), former president of the New England Legal Marketing Association, ABA book author, and Fellow of the College of Law Practice Management. She is known for her "first to market" initiatives. She is also the proud mother of one daughter, Kenna.

Jeana Goosmann, attorney
Goosmann Law
www.goosmannlaw.com
(712) 226-4000 | Jeana@goosmannlaw.com
Jeana Goosmann founded her own firm, Goosmann Law, in 2009. As the CEO and managing partner, Jeana has grown her full-service law firm to employ seven attorneys and eight support staff. Jeana is licensed in Iowa, Nebraska, and South Dakota.

Katy Goshtasbi, Branding Expert
Puris Personal Branding Solutions
purispersonalbranding.com
(949) 274-6423 | katy@purispersonalbranding.com
Katy Goshtasbi is founder and CEO of Puris Personal Branding Solutions, where she consults with law firms, corporations, and the entertainment and financial services industries on finding their unique brands and helping them to stand out and emotionally resonate with their audiences. In addition to being an international public speaker and thought-leader on the topic, she is also a former securities lawyer, in which capacity she practiced for 15 years at the SEC, in law firms, as a federal lobbyist, and as in-house counsel.

Mavis Gragg, attorney
(828) 712-4635 | attorneygragg@gmail.com
Mavis Gragg is an attorney with experience assisting clients in the financial services industry, primarily in litigation, regulatory, and compliance matters.

Carol Schiro Greenwald, consultant strategist and coach
Marketing Partners
www.greenwaldconsulting.com
(914) 834-9320 | carol@greenwaldconsulting.com
Carol Schiro Greenwald works with professional services firms and individuals to structure and implement strategically grounded, research-based, marketing, practice management, and business development initiatives. She is the author of *Build Your Practice the Logical Way—Maximize Your Client Relationships* (ABA, First Chair Press, 2012). She is also a Fellow in the College of Law Practice Management.

Afi Johnson-Parris, attorney
Ward Black Law
www.wardblacklaw.com
(336) 333-2244 | ajp@wardblacklaw.com
Afi Johnson-Parris is an attorney practicing divorce and family law and veteran's disability in Greensboro, North Carolina, with Ward Black Law. As former chair of the North Carolina Bar Association Law Practice Management Section, ABA LP Division diversity fellow, and Elon Law School Law Firm management adjunct professor, Afi has been involved with law practice management best practices on local and national levels.

Jeanne Lee, attorney/consultant
LawyerMentorCoach
www.lawyermentorcoach.com
(303) 333-2417 | Jeanne@lawyermentorcoach.com
Jeanne Lee assists her clients in leveraging their strengths in the workplace, performs communications CPR, and offers presentations that keep audiences on the edge of their seats. She is a speaker and workshop facilitator on leadership, business development, communications, and "World-Class Speaking Secrets."

Beverly Loder, marketing director
Fitch, Even, Tabin & Flannery LLP
www.fitcheven.com
(312) 629-7983 | bloder@fitcheven.com
Beverly Loder is marketing director at Fitch, Even, Tabin & Flannery LLP. She was formerly the longtime director of LPM Book Publishing for the ABA and more recently the features editor for *Law Practice* magazine. Beverly is also a Fellow in the College of Law Practice Management.

Traci Ray, executive director
Barran Liebman LLP
www.barran.com
(503) 276-2115 | tray@barran.com
Traci Ray is the executive director at Barran Liebman LLP, where she blends her enthusiasm, leadership, and solution-oriented mentality to guide the firm's management, marketing, and administration. Barran Liebman is recognized as the top employment, labor, and benefits law firm in Oregon, and Traci's number one goal is support the success of its clients, attorneys, and staff.

Dee A. Schiavelli, consultant/coach
Results Marketing for Lawyers
www.resultsmarket.com
(520) 229-3241 | dee@resultsmarket.com
Dee Schiavelli is a national business development consultant advising and coaching lawyers, helping them to effectively grow their practice. An active member of the ABA LP Division, Women Rainmakers Committee, and ABA LP Magazine Board, as well as a certified social media strategist, Dee speaks on legal marketing at bar associations, law schools, and other legal organizations.

Eleanor Southers, attorney/coach
Law Offices of Eleanor Southers/Professional Legal Coaching
www.southerslaw.net | www.professionallegalcoaching.com
(831) 466-9132 | esouthers@aol.com
Eleanor Southers is a legal coach for attorneys at all stages of their careers. Providing a wide range of experience and expertise, she is able to guide attorneys to greater success and satisfaction with their profession.

Acknowledgments

We owe thanks to many people who contributed in a variety of ways and helped make this book possible. While we served as editors, facilitators, and motivators, this book would not have happened without the extraordinary contributions of the chapter authors who conducted the interviews and the many women lawyers who graciously shared their experiences in the interviews.

Special thanks to Susan Letterman White, past chair of the LPD Women Rainmakers Board, who brought this idea to the ABA's Law Practice Division Publishing Board, and to Beverly Loder, marketing director of Fitch, Even, Tabin & Flannery, for her guidance from the beginning. Also, thanks to the ABA publishing staff editor Denise Constantine, peer reviewers, and publishing board staff for their work in guiding the book through the publishing process. And, thanks especially to our families and friends who provided unwavering support.

Introduction

This book contains a series of "stories" from women rainmakers about how they used marketing tools and methods to grow their practice. There are many books available that will list all the marketing tools, such as networking, social media, cross-selling, and so on, and give examples on where and how to use them. Some examples might be "network at organizations where your clients and prospects are," "create a LinkedIn profile and invite people you know to join your network," or "identify other services provided by your firm and work with a lawyer in that practice to cross-sell each other's practice area." We all know, though, that what we *should do* and what we *really do* are two different things. And if you are not comfortable with the implementation, you will not do it—or you will not do it well, and when it fails, you will say *it doesn't work.*

This book strives to take you beyond the theoretical approach to marketing by showing various marketing tools in action. By showing you how the marketing tool worked, rather than just telling you, we hope you gain greater insight into how you can incorporate it into your marketing efforts. The women's stories are more than just a "how to" manual on using these tools in practice to achieve marketing success. This is a call to action to move beyond barriers to implementation because these tools do work and have worked for everyday lawyers, women just like you.

In each chapter in *Marketing Success: How Did She Do That?*, we aim to give an overview of a measurable marketing tool—to explain what it is and how it is used and then to introduce the reader to stories from women rainmakers on how they used the marketing tool, what they did, how it worked, and how that action led to new business.

We are confident you will not only enjoy reading *Marketing Success: How Did She Do That?* but will be able to adapt the experiences of others to develop new business for yourself.

Chapter 1

Marketing Inside Your Practice

Afi S. Johnson-Parris

Inside Your Law Practice Overview

One of the often-ignored venues for business development is the internal one, in your own law firm and with current clients. If cultivated properly, internal referral sources of business can be the low-hanging fruit of business development. Because the other members of your firm and current clients presumably know, like, and trust you, you are already ahead of the curve when it comes to these groups making referrals or choosing you for work. The fundamentals of business development still apply, and you must make an effort to ensure that the members of your firm know what you do and who you do it for, and keep you top of mind when that work presents. You, likewise, must have that same knowledge about others in your firm so that you can direct clients to internal providers when they need services that you individually don't provide.

How Do You Focus on Internal Business Development? (Cross-selling, Teams, the Partner as Client)

Cross-selling is the term used for offering a new service to a current client. An example would be expanding work for a litigation client by adding a corporate transactional matter. Another method for

1

expanding business internally is to take a team approach to servicing clients of a particular industry or focus. The team brings together members from different practice areas to meet multiple needs, thereby increasing the services rendered. Another method is viewing partners of the firm as clients in their own right and working to participate in their business through increasing assignments or providing a niche service that their individual practice may lack.

Where Can Internal Business Development Be Used?

Women in small or large firms can benefit from bringing work into their firm, even if they are not the one to do the work. Cross-selling makes use of other lawyers and services in the firm while raising the profile of the cross-seller as a rainmaker. Women working in firms with enough lawyers to meet the specialized needs of a particular industry can benefit from the collaboration of team members to address those needs. Clients will also come to know a successful cross-seller as the trusted adviser they can go to for any problem and know that they will be matched with the appropriate problem solver. The benefit—keeping the lawyer top of mind whenever a problem arises.

The team approach allows you to target business in a specific industry, thereby creating a niche, but taking a multidisciplinary approach to serving that industry. This can be a powerful tool for marketing a firm as a one-stop solution to potential clients in an industry. Developing business from individual partners is most effective where one would not be reliant on very few partners and could have multiple "clients" that require service. An example would be offering tax advice to partners with work as varied as litigation and mergers and acquisitions. Taking the approach of finding a niche that is helpful to a broad range of practice areas or clients is key to this technique for internal business development.

This chapter examines women lawyers who have successfully built their book of business internally using the techniques just described. Their mastery of forging new relationships or capitalizing on existing relationships with colleagues and current clients will show you how these techniques can be used to become a rainmaker using resources you have at hand.

Kimberly Bullock Gatling
Partner, Smith Moore Leatherwood LLP
Intellectual Property

Kimberly Gatling has used internal business development from day one at Smith Moore Leatherwood. Initially hired as the only patent attorney in her Greensboro office, she was brought in to build a patent prosecution practice to serve a number of the firm's current clients. Then just a second-year associate, Kimberly didn't have her own book of business nor a substantial amount of work internally. She says of her strategy, "I spent a lot of time marketing myself to the attorneys in the firm and advising them of my intellectual property practice and how I could help their clients."

Initially frustrated with the lack of patent work in her early years at the firm, Kimberly found that "it ended up being a huge blessing. There was very little intellectual property work for me to handle, yet I needed a full plate of work to stay on par with my billable hours goals. Therefore, I was forced to reach out to partners about doing any type of work, whether it was IP related or not." Kimberly was not at all shy about making her willingness to work known to the partners. "I literally used to send an email every week to particular partners that I knew had work indicating that I was low on work and was willing to work on anything, even if not related to IP. Thankfully, I don't beg for work anymore, but I do use slower times to make myself (and my practice) more visible to other partners in the firm to encourage cross-marketing."

The benefit of her persistence was that she was known as a person who was ready and willing to work, and she ensured that she was top of mind and at the top of the partners' list when an assignment was being staffed. "As a result, I worked with partners with whom I ordinarily would not have worked, and I gained diverse legal experience in everything ranging from corporate to regulatory to general litigation to health care." The broad experience benefited Kimberly during times when intellectual property work was lean and helped her practice evolve so that she was positioned to be more than a patent and trademark prosecutor. "I'm more of a business partner with my clients," says Kimberly. "I can advise them on all aspects of intellectual property as well as how intellectual property meshes with their business goals and other areas of law."

A key part of Kimberly's marketing efforts was building relationships with partners throughout the firm, both locally and in other offices. She would travel to the other offices and make sure that everyone knew who she was and what she did. "I didn't always have a project that I was working on when I went to the other offices. I had to build relationships. It makes people like you and think about you." Being top of mind was just as important as her efforts to educate her colleagues on the skills she could offer to support their clients. "You need to make sure that others can spot the issue that your skills can solve and then remember that you are the person who can solve it."

Kimberly readily admits that building her practice through this method has been a gradual process during the 14 years she has been practicing. "It took seven years or more for everyone to be fully educated." She worked to identify areas where she could help and then provided advice to lawyers in those areas that would benefit their practice. For example, she helped expand the knowledge of the labor and employment attorneys on intellectual property ownership so that they could address that in employment agreements and employee handbooks. "I also listen closely when partners are talking about recruiting clients for specific areas of law (such as health care or insurance) and I make sure that I chime in to see if we can also add IP to the solicitation." In the past three years, her practice has grown in the health care field with the expanded use of electronic medical records, which increase the need for software licensing contracts. Kimberly developed this business through participating in the Health Care Group's regular meetings to educate the lawyers in the group on how she could help their clients. She also used opportunities for mixing with the firm's lawyers at events like the firm retreat as an opportunity to get to know more people in the firm and tell them about her practice and how it could help their clients.

Kimberly's educational efforts extended beyond the lawyers in her firm to firm clients as well. She joined a team of lawyers within the firm to serve and educate clients in the transportation industry. The annual seminar for clients in this industry is presented by lawyers from differing areas of the firm such as the corporate group, labor and employment, and litigation. Kimberly's intellectual property presentation at this annual seminar provided an opportunity to develop business in an area outside of the typical high-tech fields and educate these clients on how intellectual property protections are necessary for the transportation industry.

Kimberly's success with her business development efforts has been gradual, yet ongoing. "I started to feel like I had made significant headway when partners began calling me to work directly with their clients on IP matters and when partners started sending their clients directly to me. I would say it took a few years for me to establish myself as the 'point person' for certain matters." She is now able to cross-market with other partners in the firm routinely. She says, "Even when the client doesn't realize they need me, one of my partners (the primary client contact) advises them to talk to me about IP issues." Kimberly started to directly trace her efforts to new business when she began to get referrals from firm clients. This helped bolster her external firm business as a complement to what she was able to establish within the firm.

Kimberly acknowledges that a downfall to mainly focusing on internal business development is that it limits your development of your own clients such that you don't have a readily transferrable book of business. "I've now been able to develop many clients on my own, but I still consider the success of my practice to be largely dependent on serving the firm's institutional clients (i.e., other partners' clients)." One hedge of protection for her within the firm, she says, is that "no one else does what I do, and that's a plus." Having a niche makes you more likely able to develop business internally because others will seek you out for expertise they don't themselves have to meet client needs. Kimberly intends to continue to employ the same strategies that have led to her success thus far.

Kimberly does acknowledge the challenges she faces with spending adequate time and focus on marketing. "It is difficult to be deliberate and persistent about making new contacts and following up with them, especially when balancing family and getting client work done." As a busy mother, wife, and lawyer, she believes in finding the most efficient and effective ways to generate business, whether inside the firm or externally. "I have to remind myself that I have great marketing opportunities

"You need to make sure that others can spot the issue that your skills can solve and then remember that you are the person who can solve it."

in some of the activities I'm already engaged in—whether it is attending a bar-related meeting or talking with other parents at my son's swim meets." Business development inside the firm, however, still remains the most successful use of her time and effort. "A firm partner who has clients that you should be serving is an even warmer contact than the client itself. Work those warm (internal) clients that are just in the next-door office."

Kathleen Wilkinson
Partner, Wilson Elser Moskowitz Edelman & Dicker LLP

Civil Litigation: Construction, Insurance Defense, Products Liability, ADR

Kathleen Wilkinson is well positioned to be a firm rainmaker: she has professional visibility and name recognition as past chancellor of the Philadelphia Bar Association—the country's oldest bar association—and is recognized as a Pennsylvania *Super Lawyer* Top 50 Women. Her external rainmaking prowess, however, began internally as an associate working to please partner "clients" through excellent work and a willingness to take any assignment, roll up her sleeves, and dive in. As her reputation spread among the partners throughout the firm, steady work followed. She's worked with a variety of industries that are male dominated, such as aviation and construction, and used gender stereotypes to her advantage. "I was willing to go on-site and people found that impressive. I got my own steel-toe boots, safety glasses, and hard hat."

Kathleen saw her internal referrals of business grow as she gained expertise in aviation cases, which led to even more complex products liability cases being sent her way from partners throughout the firm's offices. Kathleen was then able to develop work in areas that she found interesting, like products liability, where she has defended a variety of products ranging from medical devices to heavy equipment located in steel mills. Because she was willing to write articles on medical device products liability, colleagues in the firm were aware that this was the type of work she wanted and sent her these cases when they arose. With such varied interests, today Kathleen has a diverse practice that includes defending builders and contractors in construction cases, writing insurance policies, and serving as a mediator and a judge pro tem.

Kathleen saw her success as a combination of developing unique skills that made her indispensable to the partners and communicating that she was willing to learn about the area of law and the industry. "If you have knowledge," she says, "that makes you valuable." Especially within the firm, "you need to be technically good for people to refer business to you." Kathleen was able to leverage her reputation within the firm to make partner and ultimately use that to develop business outside of the firm as well.

Admittedly, Kathleen didn't employ any intentional business development strategy as an associate. "I was just working hard to keep the firm happy and do good work." However, upon reflection on the specific things that she did to be successful in the firm, it is clear that many actions were textbook strategies for business development: building relationships, targeting a niche, and doing good work to turn partner-clients into promoters of her work. "It is important to maintain good relations with your partners," she says. Kathleen worked to develop and maintain connections by dropping in on partners she had worked with when she happened to be in the firm's other offices. She is admitted to practice in Pennsylvania and nearby New Jersey. Even when there were no active cases, she would use the downtime to discuss plans about securing other business.

Kathleen also developed a niche area of expertise. "Become the 'go to' person for that line of work," she advises. Kathleen communicated her niche expertise by requesting work that interested her, writing articles, and conducting seminars for clients. Most emphasized by Kathleen is the connection between doing good work and generating new business within the firm. "Partners were happy with my work and my ability to keep clients happy. You know you've done that if they keep coming back to you and give you work. That's when you know you've been successful with internal marketing."

Though successful early in her career developing a steady flow of business from partners satisfied with her work, Kathleen will admit to some frustrations with business development in general. "Developing business takes time," she says. Kathleen has found that "there is no direct correlation between the amount of time devoted and the business generated . . . [however,] you must market and continue to do good work at all times." The time spent, however, is not wasted. Even though time spent marketing is not counted toward her billable hours, Kathleen's firm considers it time well spent. "If you produce business as a result, the loss of billable time is made up by the billable hours brought into the firm."

As a partner, Kathleen has taken a more technical approach to business development by preparing a business plan and tracking her client development hours. This was something that she didn't do as an associate, but she has noticed a trend toward attorneys of all levels thinking differently about business development since there is more emphasis on it as part of a professional practice. By tracking her business development time spent, Kathleen is better able to see whether or not work comes from her efforts. She tries to devote some time daily to marketing, but her hours vary as there are times in her schedule that don't allow much time for marketing. Busy schedule aside, marketing is still a critical task. "It is always necessary to continue to reach out to your clients and develop business. An attorney should always try to keep her name out there." Although she formalizes her marketing approach with a business plan, Kathleen realizes that flexibility is important. "The plan you come up with may not be the one you follow. You have to be open to opportunities and be willing to deviate and follow other potential leads as well."

Specifically for young, large-firm associates who start their careers with partners as the main client, Kathleen advises, "Never say no to accepting an assignment. Always keep the partner advised of the status of the work so that you will receive more work in the future." A reputation for responsiveness and good work were always key to getting return work from partners, but the first assignment and the initial interactions with partners count. "Remember," Kathleen advises, "first impressions are lasting." Besides attracting work internally with her reputation, Kathleen was still sure to seek out assignments proactively. "A young associate should request work and not wait until he or she does not have enough work."

Displaying your expertise or developing it through self-study will also pay dividends. As mentioned, Kathleen would use her interests in certain areas of law as a catalyst for penning articles on the topic. "As one moves up in the associate ranks, the associate should volunteer to write articles or conduct seminars of interest to clients." The benefits of this strategy are many. Writing the article or teaching clients about the important points of an area of law expand your knowledge base and expertise. You can transition this knowledge and expertise into a niche and make yourself indispensable to the partner on the matter.

As Kathleen reached the ranks of equity partners in the firm, her focus on internal business development shifted toward external clients. Although the focus was different, many actions remained the same. Kathleen works to build relationships with clients and colleagues within the bench and the bar who can serve as referral sources.

Her term as chancellor of the Philadelphia Bar Association in 2013 provided an opportunity to merge her professional activities with marketing efforts. She deftly found a dual purpose for her involvement by using bar events and programming as an opportunity to develop and nurture relationships with clients that she would invite to these events. She also built relationships with other lawyers on a broader scale than ever before.

Due to the consensus-building skills she learned while working her way up to bar chancellor, Kathleen has been serving as a judge pro tem and a special discovery master, and has developed an alternative dispute resolution practice. "I now view my business generation as possible through other lawyers and my bar connections so my strategy has changed."

Much of Kathleen's marketing success and the reputation that she has gained in the legal community originated from the foundation she built with her first client base, inside her firm. She turned those partner-clients into contacts within the external clients and then nurtured them. Kathleen herself acknowledges, "I reached success by forming personal relationships with clients, working very hard to do great work, and then continuing to nourish the relationship." The bedrock of business development for her appears to be consistently based on relationships and good work. This is a formula that every woman attorney can strive to apply to her career to become a successful rainmaker.

Therese Pritchard
Chair, Bryan Cave LLP
Securities Enforcement and White Collar Criminal Defense

Therese Pritchard has pursued internal business from the very beginning of her tenure at Bryan Cave through a strategy of education and outreach. Out of her 35 years of practicing law, Therese has been in private practice for 19 of those years. During her transitions from in-house counsel and government service to private practice, Therese had to become adept at generating business instead of relying on the work being readily available. When asked how she approached marketing herself among her colleagues when she joined the firm in 1999, Therese replies, "I hit the road—I visited our offices and made presentations over lunch. I got to know partners across the firm so that when their clients had a problem, they would know I was available."

Bryan Cave is a large, multinational firm of more than 1,000 lawyers, which provides fertile ground for internal business development. The challenge for Therese, however, has been getting the word out about what she does and the capabilities of the firm in her area. "In a firm of our size, it's hard for everyone to know who does what. When I hear about an opportunity that we didn't pursue because a partner didn't realize we had the right expertise, that can be frustrating."

Therese's target for outreach began with a natural sector of the firm for her area of practice focused on protecting businesses and business professionals—the corporate group. "As a securities regulatory lawyer, I attended corporate retreats, because the corporate group was often the first to learn that there was a problem within a company." While she formed relationships with the corporate attorneys throughout the firm, she provided advice and education on how their clients could be impacted by securities regulation. The corporate attorneys' awareness of how Therese could help paved the way for her to generate business among their clients and cross-sell another service to existing clients. Therese's efforts required more than just one interaction and steady follow-up. She notes, "I consistently kept the corporate group sensitized to our securities litigation and enforcement capabilities so that we would have a better shot at getting that work."

Therese also had to persist against the belief of her colleagues that their clients didn't need her services. "There was some skepticism early on because some of the partners didn't believe their clients had the type of problems that I handled." Therese was able to add examples to her tools of education and outreach by showing partners her capabilities with external clients. "As they saw me doing work that I generated myself, they started thinking of me when they learned of clients' problems." Her volume of internal business still took time to increase. As Therese recalls, "It took a few years—longer than I expected." Yet Therese knew she had achieved success when other lawyers in the firm began to call her about the problems that their clients were having.

Her work with her own external clients added an important piece to her strategy of education and outreach—creditability. In order to be successful with internal business development, "you have to gain a certain level of creditability within a firm of this size," Therese says.

"Eventually, you become known by word of mouth—your partners start marketing you internally by telling other partners about you." Doing good work and displaying your expertise with the clients that you have can help create buzz, even within your own firm, so that your partners become promoters of you and your work. This internal word of mouth can work in the same manner as it would with external business development and help you market effectively to get new clients.

The growth in Therese's practice can be attributed to marketing. "Marketing is time well spent," she says. "When I was practicing full time, on average I devoted a few hours a week to marketing. It was not consistent every week—when I was absorbed in a big case, I might not do any marketing; at other times, I might spend days preparing and participating in panels at conferences."

Therese will put her internal business development skills to use for other members of the firm in her role as the chair of Bryan Cave, the first woman in this position in the firm's history. She describes part of her role as a marketer for the firm. "It's not really about building my own practice as much as building the firm's business overall." As other women consider which strategies they should take in developing their own business within their firms, Therese advises that "they shouldn't be shy about talking about their expertise, their victories, and their prior experience. It can be hard for women to brag." When women come to view this self-promotion as an important part of their marketing efforts, who knows what success can follow.

Betsy G. Ramos
Partner, Capehart & Scatchard, PA
Litigation

Betsy Ramos's business development strategy has evolved over her 30-some years of practice; she first pursued internal work from other partners and is now expanding her business through cross-selling and team marketing.

Betsy moved to diversify her marketing strategy in an effort to develop more of her own individual clients. "I used to say my best clients were my partners, but at some point, you can't get your own clients that way and grow your practice independently."

As a litigator, Betsy faced the challenge of cases being a singular engagement instead of multiple matters that provided a steady stream of work. "For many years, I focused on pursuing higher rate work—business litigation and estate litigation. It is difficult to develop either of these areas directly because neither involves repeat litigation." Working internally to develop this business started with targeting her partners who had current clients with litigation needs. "I fostered good relationships with my business and estate partners by being available when needed to handle sometimes emergent or time-consuming matters, working well with their clients, as well as being successful in handling the matter." Her good work led to developing a referral network of partners within the firm. "My success, whether through litigating the matter to conclusion or settlement, encouraged my partners to continue to refer these types of matters to me as they arose." As she continued to receive referrals from her internal contacts, Betsy was encouraged to persist in her marketing efforts. Her success felt very rewarding.

Over the past two years, Betsy began to broaden her internal marketing strategy by not just taking on litigation work for current firm clients whenever a case arose, but by developing new services for those clients within the litigation context. She actively pursued volume clients, those who have lower rates but higher volume of work. Betsy's shift was intentionally designed to increase her book of business rather than just increasing the revenue she generated. "This would give me more of my own clients and let me be less dependent on others to refer work to me." She recognized, however, that this strategy was just one of many she needed to employ. "I used a combination of internal cross-selling, as well as marketing on my own."

Betsy targeted firm institutional clients to cross-sell her litigation expertise to what had traditionally been nonlitigation practice areas. Her first target was the firm's workers' compensation clients. Betsy's workers' compensation partners introduced her to their clients' risk managers, and she began to form relationships to do their liability work. This became a new line of business for her firm. She began to attend the firm seminars held for workers' compensation clients and association events for workers' compensation claims professionals. Betsy was then able to market her litigation services to other workers' compensation professionals and increase her recognition among those in this industry.

Turning an interest into an area of expertise is a method Betsy recommends for cross-selling to get more work within the firm. If others know your interests and what you do, it can lead to more work. Betsy advises, "Write an article and distribute it within the firm, speak at firm meetings, interact with colleagues at firm events and make it known that you do or are interested in a certain type of work so people can refer internally instead of outside the firm."

As Betsy points out, there is more to cross-selling than just gaining an introduction to the clients of others. "There has to be a trust developed with your fellow partners that you will get along with their clients, that you will handle any referred matters successfully, and that you will not try to interfere in any way with their relationship with that client. That is really the secret of obtaining referrals within your firm." The trust between partners that is necessary for success in cross-selling comes from relationships that have been developed and nurtured. "People only give business to people they know; that's true internally just as well as externally," says Betsy. The process for internal business development closely mirrors what a lawyer must do to develop business externally. Betsy firmly believes that "it's really no different from getting outside clients; in both arenas you have to cultivate trust, pay your dues, and show you will handle clients successfully. You have to invest time and effort into those relationships just like you would an outside relationship."

Positioning herself to take over a client relationship when a senior partner transitioned his practice was another internal source of business for Betsy. She had worked for many years as an associate for this partner, and at the end of his career he handed off the client to Betsy because she had proved her ability to handle the work. This source of clients, however, has limitations as it tends to be more likely suited for attorneys of sufficient stature and experience. Rather than a business development technique, inheriting clients is more like a natural benefit of the relationship-building and dues-paying efforts successful rainmakers like Betsy often employ.

Betsy has also found that internal success in business development can be self-replicating by building your reputation in the firm as a rainmaker and a trusted representative to interact with firm clients. "By demonstrating that you can successfully market to others' clients, it encourages your partners to invite you to their marketing events. Just as you see opportunity in other partners who have a book of business, they can see opportunity in you." As your success begets success, Betsy notes, "you can then be in a position to refer to others and help cross-sell your own clients to others, which can only help solidify your relationship with your fellow partners, with whom you are trying to cross-sell to their clients."

The team approach to marketing is often an internal effort geared at external current and potential clients. Particularly for Betsy, business litigation had been difficult to generate with any consistency. Her goal was "to develop relationships with businesses or individuals in hope that, if litigation arises, they will retain you." This method alone, however, was not enough to maintain a robust business.

Betsy and her partners tried the team approach by hosting a business symposium targeting business clients. She and other partners in the firm used the symposium as an opportunity to present to these potential clients and to maintain relationships with current clients that had also been invited. Their efforts met with frustrating results. Betsy didn't get new clients or new business. Reflecting on their approach, Betsy says, "You can't just put on one seminar to make it effective." She acknowledges that many factors were at play with the symposium's lack of success, and it could have been a number of things like the topic or the right mix of target audience. "There's a lot more that you need to focus on—knowing what clients are going to be there and what type of work they have that you want and asking partners to introduce you to their clients so you can meet and then follow up." The follow-up perhaps was the missing ingredient. Betsy believes that her interactions at the symposium were not as effective because of insufficient efforts to engage her contacts multiple times after the symposium concluded. "I didn't know to do that follow-up," she says.

The symposium experience was a lesson learned and one not at all wasted on Betsy. Understanding what didn't work, she then sought out ways to determine what did. First, she targeted partners in her firm who were good at marketing and business development and then had conversations with them about their techniques. One partner had successfully used the seminar technique to generate business with existing and potential clients, and Betsy queried him about his methods. "I realized," she said, "I can do this too!" With her partner's advice in hand, Betsy hosted another seminar targeting workers' compensation clients. "I got 44 people to come and got two clients out of that." In this instance, Betsy was sure to capitalize on the seminar by working to maintain contact and build relationships with the attendees long after the seminar was completed. "There's a lot of follow-up involved," she noted.

As Betsy has honed her business development skills, she has also gotten more aggressive and formal with her business development strategy. At the beginning of last year, she developed a marketing plan and spent about 150 to 200 hours on marketing during the year. When she reviewed the plan the next January, she realized that she had met every goal she set. Her success has only worked to encourage her to continue her efforts, and she has crafted another plan to advance her business objectives. "Having concrete goals and objectives really helped me focus on my marketing and I feel directly contributed to its success." The additional attention to marketing, she believes, "directly resulted in two new clients, additional leads I can follow up on this year, as well as enhanced relationships, both externally and internally, with my fellow partners, which I expect will pay off in the future."

The evolution of Betsy's business development strategy from a singular focus on partners as clients to an array of ways to develop business from teams and cross-selling illustrates her best advice to other women lawyers: "Diversify your efforts so that they are a combination of working with your fellow partners to cross-sell (after you have gained their trust to do so), along with your own solo marketing efforts." A strength of her strategy is the ability to secure her own clients rather than just generate revenue. "My best advice is to use a combination of marketing efforts and not to rely on any one strategy. This way you are not solely reliant on others in developing clients and can develop your own clients."

Conclusion

The similarity between the techniques used to develop business internally and externally is striking. The advantage of honing your marketing skills internally, in what should be a more comfortable environment, can profoundly impact your readiness to use those skills outside of the firm. A consistent message in each woman's story was the importance of relationships. They matter. Fostering those relationships within your firm not only supports your business development efforts but also enhances your professional development at the firm.

All four women benefited from gaining expertise in a niche or targeting a niche to provide legal service that met client demands. Increasing the value of what you provide—both its excellence and its rarity—is a good method for securing your position when the bulk of your work comes from other partners rather than your own clients.

Teams that hunt for business together also benefit from individual team members who provide expertise to the group that no one else has. Targeting current firm clients to meet an unmet need expands the client's business with the firm through cross-selling and benefits from the niche approach as well.

For any woman lawyer who imagined marketing as a big-budget undertaking or cold-calling sales pitches, the reality of what can be done to develop business, right in your own firm, should be encouraging. Kimberly, Kathleen, Therese, and Betsy have varied backgrounds and practices; however, their common ability to capitalize on the resources within their firms to market and build their practice provides a road map for others to follow, no matter how varied their terrain.

Chapter 2

Networking

Anne Collier

What is networking? Networking is an attitude, an approach to life. It's not a "thing to do." Rather, it's a way of relating to the people around you and creating mutually supportive relationships within your communities. You know others for their expertise and they know you for your expertise.

You ask, how do they do it—how do women build their own business through networking? This chapter briefly tells the story of four women's use of networking as a business development tool. Their strategies differ and are governed in large part by practice area and personality. While the women themselves are each remarkable and successful, their stories suggest that by thinking strategically, prioritizing, persevering, and leveraging personal strengths, any woman can build her own practice through networking.

Why is networking a premier, if not *the* premier, business development tool? It's because, as Jeffrey Gitomer says in his *Little Black Book of Connections:*

> All things being equal, people want to do business with their friends
>
> . . . AND . . .
>
> All things not being equal, people *still* want to do business with their friends.

A "friendship" with clients and referral sources is a little different than the friendship you have with the woman you shared sleepovers with in second grade and then hangovers with in college. Well, not really. The key elements are the same: you have a relationship built up over time so that you trust each other, you know you have each other's back, and you are a resource to and help for each other.

Jessica Adler

Owner, Law Offices of Jessica E. Adler
Domestic Relations

The instinctive networker. From the get-go—from the time she moved to Washington, DC, in 2000—Jessica Adler networked. She didn't have a job and she didn't know anyone. She asked friends to connect her to their friends in DC. She met these friends of friends for coffee, and they connected her to others. And so it began.

Jessica networked to land her first job and then to get her second job. In addition to instinctively networking, Jessica benefited from having good mentors and role models who encouraged her to get involved and to network strategically. Her first boss suggested she join the Women's Bar Association (WBA) of DC. She did and became very involved, so much so that she was elected president of the organization for the 2013–2014 term. In February 2006, she started her own firm and began networking to find clients who needed her help in domestic relations, divorce, custody, child custody, and prenuptial agreements.

Networking Is Not Work

Jessica has always enjoyed being around other people and considers herself an extrovert—she thrives on other people's energy. Starting out, Jessica used networking more as a social development tool rather than a business development strategy. Her boss's suggestion to join the WBA helped open her eyes to her own natural inclination to meet new people and build both personal and professional relationships with them. "I will say I didn't like [networking at] first," she admits. "I mean, it was always very awkward to walk into a room where you don't know anyone, so it took a few times to get comfortable, and then I grew to really enjoy it. Especially with the WBA [events] . . . I'm never nervous now because I always know people."

From the beginning, Jessica's strategy was to reach out to people who knew people, "latching onto them at social events," she jokes. Two lawyer friends, in particular, served as her guides, introducing her around at events that they thought would help her to build her professional relationships. "At first, even extroverts can find it difficult to attend events where they don't know anyone," Jessica says. This is especially the case in groups where there are many cliques. Becoming more comfortable with the process of networking and group dynamics was certainly a challenge that she had to overcome.

By the end of her first year in DC, she had attended enough events to develop confidence in her networking ability and her natural instinct to meet and get to know people. Now, the anxiety is gone and she feels comfortable going to events, even those where she doesn't know anyone. Her advice is simple: "Keep going; you get more comfortable."

Now she pays it forward by mentoring and connecting others. "I try to do everything I would want other people to do for me, with every law student or young lawyer who contacts me to go to coffee or lunch."

Her networking strategy has evolved and perhaps even a little accidentally. At first, she networked just to make friends. Now, she is much more deliberate in where she invests her time. Thus, while she admits that she is involved in more organizations than most, she makes time to be very involved with four or five key organizations rather than joining ten organizations and spreading herself too thin.

Realistic Expectations

Intentional from the beginning of her networking journey, Jessica was careful to create a set of realistic expectations about what her networking would yield. This helped her avoid frustrations she had seen her friends and colleagues experience.

She attends numerous events and realizes that it takes time to build relationships. Others are less patient; they attend one event and then complain it was a waste because they didn't get any business. Jessica says that it's rare to walk away from one event with new business. She tells the story of a colleague, a financial planner whom she advised to attend a Women's Bar Association event. Afterward, the financial planner called her exasperated, complaining that "no business came of it." Jessica told her, "Well, business doesn't happen overnight."

She knows that results are not immediate. In her experience, it's the people she's known for years who are more likely to refer business to her over time. She knows and accepts that not every person is going to call her. She figures, "The more my name gets out, the better it is for me." That is a lot and enough for Jessica.

For Jessica, it's a matter of math and inputs. New business, for her, is a function of the number of affinity organizations to which she belongs, how many people she meets, how well she gets to know them, and how long they have known one another. In this regard, the bar year 2013–2014 was a big year for Jessica and networking. She spent at least ten hours a week on average engaged in activities that expanded and reinforced her relationships with others—her network. She admits that the amount of time was unusually high, even for her. Being the WBADC president meant additional projects, lunch and dinner meetings, events several times a week, and conference calls.

Lawyer to Lawyer

Nowhere are the results of her networking more evident than among Jessica's connections within the legal community. "I do interact with a lot of lawyers, and lawyers know a lot of lawyers, and I think that gives me a direct benefit for getting a lot of lawyer referrals."

As one measure of this strategy's effectiveness, she points to the number of hits and clicks she's received on Martindale-Hubbell's referral, a referral service catering mostly to other lawyers. She's seen far more activity from this site than the more consumer-oriented Lawyers.com. This is very different than most domestic relations lawyers' experiences and reflects her heavy investment in getting to know other lawyers.

Jessica's clients come to her in different ways. Most often, clients are referred by someone she knows and has met on many occasions—not just once. "The WBA has certainly [led to] a lot of clients, but it's not one particular event, it's relationship building over a period of years," Jessica reiterates.

Occasionally, the referral source is someone who has heard her teach a CLE course or speak at another event. Finally, clients find Jessica on the Internet. Although she's never met them or been referred by someone she knows, they tell Jessica the reason they called her is that they liked her bio.

When it comes to getting referrals from existing clients, Jessica takes a more passive approach. Rather than put "the ask" on clients for referrals, which is counter to advice from business development seminars, she assumes that happy clients will happily refer her.

With such a high-touch, high-intensity strategy, Jessica has had to find the right balance between life and work—one that allows for plenty of networking. Being a solo practitioner, Jessica can manage her caseload so that she is not in the office 60 hours a week, which would be too much given her commitment to and enjoyment of networking. Her work-life balance isn't necessarily about being at home a lot. For her, it's balancing networking, which she enjoys, with the actual work, which luckily she also enjoys.

When Jessica's not networking with other lawyers, she enthusiastically connects with members of affinity groups she belongs to, such as the Anti-Defamation League, where she serves on the Executive Committee of the Regional Board. She is also on the board for the local University of Wisconsin Alumni Chapter, and she does a fair amount of networking in the Jewish community. She was on the steering committee of a local synagogue professional division and was involved with the Jewish Federation of Greater Washington. While other lawyers are a good source of referrals, they are not her only source. Remember, she moved to Washington not knowing anyone, so she joined groups to meet people and make friends.

Notwithstanding her busy schedule, Jessica is always game for other opportunities. A couple of years ago, for example, she was asked if she would coteach a CLE course on drafting separation agreements with Linda Ravdin, an authority in the field. Jessica was flattered and jumped at the chance. "I think . . . being a smart business person [means] trying to always say 'yes' to opportunities."

She continues, "When I was approached and asked if I would consider being Women's Bar president, I had to think about it, but you need to have a positive attitude and say 'yes,' because these are things that are going to further your career. The same thing with the CLE, it's a lot of work but very rewarding and a lot of fun, as well."

Jessica's Advice

Jessica advises other lawyers to target their networking. Luckily, with family law, anyone she meets, she says, is a potential client or referral source. Once a lawyer figures out where to meet the people she wants and needs to meet, she needs to "keep going and keep adding." Jessica also recommends that "you try to do things that you enjoy because if [going to events] is a chore, you are less likely to do it and it's going to make it a lot harder to network effectively." She adds, "Don't stop, even if it's a chore at first."

Jessica estimates that she gets 75 percent of her business from networking. She plans to continue networking and get involved in other organizations. Jessica aspires to be the DC Bar president someday, and after her tenure as the Women's Bar Association of DC president, she will try to join the Board of Governors for the DC Bar.

Jessica believes that the benefits of networking far exceed any downside. She observes that many lawyers sit complacently at their desks because they already have a job. What they don't realize is that one day they will either want another job or need to get clients. Both require knowing people. Thus, networking is important to do even when busy.

Jessica advises everyone to have an elevator pitch—a concise statement about your services that will help your contacts determine whom they should refer to you. She notes that almost everyone who knows her also knows what she does and would know to refer her if the right person came along. She is convinced this is why she gets so many referrals. Her advice: "Make people aware of what you are doing, in a nice way." If they want to refer, they will, she says.

Volunteering to help at events is a great strategy for proving yourself, for getting to know others, and for helping them to recognize you, especially if you are shy. That's what she did when she first got involved in the Women's Bar Association. She remembers, "I joined the Annual Dinner Committee because I didn't know anyone; I figured that would be a good place I could go to meetings and I'd belong there, versus showing up at a networking event feeling lost."

Don't forget about how you look, she cautions. Her mother's advice: "'Dress the part.' This means dress as though you are a success, invest in clothes, and always look good so that people remember you that way." Finally, it's really important "to keep at it, and to keep trying, remembering that it gets more comfortable as you go along."

Jessica does acknowledge, however, that networking is really awkward for some and difficult for others who are unable to attend events due to child care responsibilities. In these cases, she recommends teaching, writing, doing what's possible to make a name for oneself. The key is for each person to figure out what works for her.

Jessica's Top 10 Networking Tips

1. Get your name out through networking via events, CLE, and the like.
2. Make time to be very involved with four or five key organizations rather than joining ten organizations and spreading yourself too thinly.
3. Volunteer to help at events. It's a great strategy for proving oneself, for getting to know others, and for feeling like you belong.

Jessica's Top 10 Networking Tips *(continued)*

4. Remember, business doesn't happen overnight. It's relationship building over a period of years.
5. Doing great work is part of your business development. Satisfied clients will happily refer you.
6. When you are new to a community or network, ask others to introduce you.
7. Being a smart businessperson means saying "yes" to opportunities.
8. Try to do things that you enjoy, because if going to events is a chore, you are less likely to do it.
9. Keep going—you will get more comfortable.
10. The key is for each person to figure out what works for her.

Celia Roady

Partner, Morgan, Lewis & Bockius LLP

Tax

Networking in the Early Years

Knowledge, craft, good client relations. Celia Roady represents tax-exempt organizations and members of their affiliated entities, which sometimes include for-profit organizations, partnerships, or other ventures in which they may participate. Her work focuses on tax and governance issues affecting tax-exempt organizations, including charities, foundations, colleges and universities, museums, and other nonprofit organizations.

Celia has networked since she was a "baby lawyer" in the mid 1970s. In the early stages of her career, Celia's networking strategy centered on building the quality of her legal work—she was always looking for ways to improve her craft. With this in mind, she joined the ABA Section of Taxation because she knew it would bring her into contact with many of the nation's finest tax lawyers. "The early stages [of networking] were focused on becoming a skilled lawyer, and being part of the ABA Tax Section really helped me be a good lawyer."

And that's how Celia began building her reputation. She started with the ABA Tax Section's committee on tax-exempt organizations. She attended meetings and took advantage of opportunities to speak and work on projects, both of which allowed her to get to know many senior lawyers in the field. "My early networking was . . . not so much [with] potential clients as getting a head start [on] building a reputation in my field with other lawyers."

Celia notes that the ABA is much more welcoming to young lawyers than in years past. She admits it can be a bit hard at first to get involved. It's worth persevering, Celia says, because the lawyer will benefit both professionally and personally. She also recommends joining the relevant section of their local mandatory or voluntary bar—in her case, the DC Bar Tax Section. This is because local bars are smaller than the ABA and often provide a more inviting atmosphere where young lawyers can advance more easily through the leadership ranks.

Even in the early days, Celia focused on developing good relationships with clients. She figured out that one of her challenges—a challenge most young lawyers still face—was to be seen as somebody who is really valuable to a client. This was especially difficult when a client was someone old enough to be the lawyer's father, which was more of an issue when she started practicing law in the 1970s.

Developing this kind of professional rapport is important because the more senior lawyers must see the clients as willing to take, and pay for, advice from junior lawyers in a firm. "[Clients] have to be seen as willing to take advice from you and willing to believe that you're worth spending their money on, as opposed to getting the advice from just the more senior lawyers at your firm."

Getting clients to have confidence in the legal advice she provided, Celia admits, was a challenge. Her secret was—and still is— preparation. As a young lawyer, Celia learned to prepare for client calls by creating an outline of the points she was going to make, how the call might go, and what she needed to accomplish on the call. She even thought through the questions the client might ask and how she would answer. While it may sound obvious, she encourages younger lawyers at her firm to prepare in a similar manner.

Her strategy worked. By the time Celia worked her way to senior-level associate, clients had started finding their way to her, and she took over primary responsibility for some of the exempt-organization clients at the firm.

Networking Today

Celia is still involved with the ABA Tax Section, which continues to be an incredibly valuable experience for her. In addition to the ABA, her networking has evolved in other ways. Now she chairs

Georgetown Law Center's conference called "Representing and Managing Tax-Exempt Organizations." She's enjoyed the experience so much that she's chaired this premier conference in her field for nearly 20 years. And, along the way, she has expanded her network to include many of the speakers and attendees.

The conference is a good networking experience for everybody, Celia notes. She tries to ensure that the conference is of interest to both lawyers at firms as well as in-house counsel. As a consequence, quite a few in-house lawyers attend. She believes that associating with a regular conference, especially if the lawyer can present or organize it, is a good networking and reputation-building activity. "I have gotten business, not a ton of business, but I have gotten business from people who attend the conference, and I think it's helped with name recognition."

In years past, Celia has spoken at other tax conferences. She participated in the legal counsel section of the American Society of Association Executives (ASAE), where she helped to plan and speak at ASAE conferences on matters within her expertise, such as nonprofit governance. She notes that presenting and being involved with ASAE exposed her to potential clients—those who manage associations and are likely faced with problems she can solve.

Being a resource for others, Celia says, is also a good networking practice. She is always willing to spend time helping younger lawyers, other lawyers she meets through the ABA, and accountants. This is often reciprocal: when no one at the firm is an expert and she wants a "reality check," she'll call a colleague from the ABA Tax Section and bounce the idea off of him or her. In this regard, she says, "I try to reciprocate . . . and always be willing and accessible if an accountant [or another lawyer] wants to call me and bounce an idea off [me]. I think lawyers shouldn't always be thinking every piece of advice they give has to be turned into something billable or they're not going to do it."

Celia also enjoys the personal benefits of networking for business. Many of her colleagues outside of her firm have become close friends and she is able to see them regularly at ABA Tax Section meetings.

The Importance of Being Patient

Like Jessica, Celia hasn't been frustrated by networking; she's always had realistic expectations. She knows that not every bit of networking is going to lead to work immediately. "It's kind of like you cast out a lot of bread on the water and something is going to come back. You just have to be prepared to spend a lot of time."

Moreover, in tax, lawyers will often handle a problem on a one-time basis. Celia finds ways to stay in touch with clients by sending them articles and letting them know about future developments in the law that seem relevant to what she knows about them, even if they haven't called her and asked about the issue. She also makes it a point to repurpose materials she's created for conferences. She shares her outlines and other materials she prepared via her mailing list and sends out materials via the firm's "law flashes" to help clients and others who might be interested. Sharing materials and resources is an integral part of her networking because it builds name recognition, reminds clients of her work, and reinforces that she is a trusted resource.

The "Happy Point"

As a senior associate, Celia began to build her business through referrals. Building a client base, however, doesn't happen overnight. It takes time—years of steady building, in fact—for business to become substantial. She reflects that "if you . . . build a good reputation so that you're . . . known in your field, then you can get to the point—the happy point, really—where people contact you that you have never heard of, that you don't know."

Ultimately, if a lawyer does a good job networking and building a reputation, the business comes to the lawyer rather than the lawyer having to develop it. At least, that is what Celia has experienced.

Celia believes that today, with the Internet, all of a lawyer's presentations, speeches, articles, conferences, and reputation as an expert are even more important. "Your reputation precedes you because people, before they ever meet you, check you out online and they'll see what you have done."

Thus, because clients can often determine who the top lawyers in a particular field are, a lawyer must establish herself as a top lawyer. The reason it is necessary to build a reputation as a top lawyer is so that a general counsel has no qualms about hiring the lawyer. Building a solid reputation makes it easier for general counsels to hire the lawyer because they know they won't be criticized, even if the lawyer doesn't "hit a home run."

Still, Celia's best source of business has been referrals from existing general counsel clients who have a friend or a colleague who is looking for a lawyer. Celia has also gotten a lot of business when a general counsel or a lawyer she has worked with at one organization moves to another organization. "I have found that just being a really good lawyer, doing the best work that I can for every client and finding a way to distinguish myself in working with these clients, has really been the best source of referrals through the years."

Not Always Networking

Celia does not subscribe to the school of thought that everything a lawyer does is a networking opportunity. Celia says, "It's been important for me to have my own personal life that doesn't revolve around feeling like there is a conscious need to network [all of the time]."

Accordingly, she's never felt compelled to tell the parents on the sidelines of a soccer game what she does, even though, admittedly, neighbors and other parents can be potential sources of networking or business. Notwithstanding, every once in a while, Celia is pleasantly surprised when a personal interaction does lead to business.

Celia's Advice

If a lawyer wants referrals and other networking opportunities, "The first thing you should do is really work on being as good a lawyer as you can be," she advises.

This is how lawyers get referrals and other opportunities. A lawyer has to know the law, be able to write well, and think about the clients' needs and perspectives. "Young lawyers," Celia continues, "need to learn how to develop relationships with their peers who work for their clients. They need to take their peers to lunch occasionally and get to know them on a personal level. As the young lawyer 'grows up,' the in-house young lawyer will grow up and move up too."

Celia also recommends that lawyers keep in touch with clients by sending them new rulings and the like, including materials prepared for conferences. Young associates, she says, need to flag these issues for partners.

Celia advises young partners to become expert in their fields and to invest time in developing their reputations and in finding mentors who can help them. A great example concerns a younger lawyer she asked to update and publish an article on how to survive an Internal Revenue Services (IRS) audit that Celia had written a number of years ago. Not long after the article was published, a prospective client met with Celia and this younger lawyer, having already Googled them to learn about the firm. The associate's article was right at the top of the list, under her own name, not Celia's. "[The associate's article] was a great introduction and helped get the business," Celia says.

Finally, and perhaps most importantly, regardless of level, a lawyer must have impact and be seen as an authority and contributor. Celia tells her young associates, "It's not enough to have it in your head, you have to communicate it, and you have to go to meetings [and conferences] and participate."

When in meetings, therefore, she recommends that the associate have a couple of valuable points in mind to add to the conversation. It's not enough that the lawyer's colleagues know the young lawyer's thoughts on a matter; clients and others outside the firm must also know. Preparation is critical.

When the lawyer is more senior, the expectations are higher and different. The lawyer must be able to walk into a room and take command of the meeting. In Celia's experience, "Victory goes to the lawyer who is most prepared."

As she learned early on: This means preparing by thinking about what the meeting is all about, what needs to be accomplished, what needs to happen, and the solutions the lawyers are going to offer.

Celia's Top 10 Networking Tips

1. Use networking to learn from other lawyers.
2. Build your reputation early, even before you are thinking about having your own clients.
3. Join the ABA or your local bar association and work on projects and presentations.
4. Do great work for existing clients—they are your best source of referrals.
5. Stay in touch with anyone you've done work with, especially your peers and clients.
6. Chair or organize a regular conference.
7. Repurpose materials that you've prepared for conferences; send materials to clients and others who are interested.
8. Help colleagues outside the firm by giving them a "reality check" when they ask for it.
9. Be patient and be prepared to spend a lot of time networking.
10. Prepare and participate in meetings. Take charge and be heard.

Rita Cavanagh

Retired Partner, Latham & Watkins, LLP

Tax

Serendipitous networking, a nonlinear matrix. Rita Cavanagh specialized in tax controversy, which is the process of resolving differences with the Internal Revenue Services at an administrative level within the IRS or before a court in litigation, before retiring from Latham & Watkins, LLP, in January 2014. From the vantage of "having done it," Rita reflects on her experience building a successful practice: "[There isn't] a single way [to build a practice, and] it's not linear either . . . it's a matrix. It's a small world in some ways, and that's important to realize."

As an example of the nonlinear matrix, Rita reflects on her experience with four women copanelists at the Federal Bar Association in late 2013. Rita had known three of them for years. More significantly, she had worked with three of them at one point, either in a law firm or in government.

Rita explains how the matrix is created: you and others move between firms or in and out of private practice, the government, and even in-house positions. You get to know each other, you work together—often representing different interests—and you develop a relationship and trust. It is because of the unpredictable nature of your path, intertwined with others' paths, that the road to a successful private practice is not a straight line. Rather, it is the result of the matrix you've created for yourself by making strategic career moves.

The 80/20 Principle

Rita uses the 80/20 Principle as a management tool. She learned this in her prelaw life as an economist. The 80/20 Principle is part of a management-by-objective system and means one should spend 80 percent of one's time on the truly important work—the billable work—and then 20 percent on routine or other work. To Rita, this means a lawyer focuses 80 percent of her time on client matters and looking for client work via pitches and the like. The remaining 20 percent of "professional time" should be spent thinking about one's career and creating the matrix. Early in her career, for example, Rita was involved with her law school alumni association, first as secretary and then as president. This gave her the opportunity to take a leadership position and be involved at her law school, which was a great way to network with her colleagues.

Rita recommends that lawyers apply this management-by-objective strategy and 80/20 Principle throughout their careers. In this regard, Rita observes that lawyers need to use different methods to develop business at different stages in their careers. They need to have enough presence of mind to seek advice from others in their practice area or firm if they are not sure what they should be doing.

For example, by the time a lawyer is a fifth- or sixth-year associate, Rita recommends developing a business plan so that the lawyer has goals to measure herself against and can give herself a "little report card." The benefit of creating one's business plan is that the lawyer must think "systematically about goals and objectives, including those on the business development side."

The plan must be specific: "It is a management-by-objective system. If the plan is to write an article every other year, the lawyer has to be on the alert for finding topics. The plan may include getting involved in two or three pitches a year, even if it's only to help put the materials together and the lawyer never get[s] face-to-face with [prospective clients]."

She advises associates to think broadly in creating a plan and to push themselves.

Get Involved

The 80/20 Principle is about devoting 20 percent of your professional time to getting involved. Because Rita is a tax controversy expert, she developed substantive expertise on a case-by-case, as-needed basis. Consequently, she looked to her partners, whose practices were far more industry specific, for introductions to trade associations and opportunities that were industry specific.

Another strategy she used was to put on seminars with colleagues for the Tax Executives Institute and other similar organizations. She notes that the accounting firms are very prolific in this regard: they will often host annual or biannual seminars for entire industries, bringing in a whole collection of industry experts in an attempt to educate and woo existing and prospective clients. The challenge is that efforts to put on a conference or a seminar are all nonbillable time, and when lawyers are younger, they "feel very stressed, but they've got to make some room for it. Even if it's just on what I call the 80/20 Principle, meaning the lawyer must allocate some time to networking."

Networking also includes building relationships within a lawyer's firm. Like other young associates, Rita focused on her work, devoting almost all of her time to researching and writing. And, like other associates, she found the practice in the early years to be a "bit isolating." This changed when she became involved in the Associates Committee and then later the Finance Committee at her firm. The latter committee consisted of partners and associates from different practice groups, so being involved really helped her get to know her colleagues at Latham.

This kind of committee work is important because it enables lawyers to meet others outside their practice area. Moreover, other lawyers get to know the young associate—how articulate she is, the way she thinks, and what she's like to work with. "You're going to get a profile within a firm to some degree, and all of that is helpful because the partners and associates—we all talk to each other."

Rita further notes the importance of the "social emollient" that occurs when lawyers are together in social settings.

Rita recommends that midlevel associates be involved in at least one bar association, such as the ABA, as well as their local mandatory and perhaps one of the local voluntary bars. In the tax field in DC, for example, there is the local DC Bar Tax Section, the ABA Tax Section, and the Federal Bar Association. The latter presents a good opportunity to meet government lawyers, which is important for lawyers with a regulatory practice.

Rita notes that even though she rarely presented in the latter years of her practice, she attended meetings to see both colleagues in other firms and government agency employees. She never knew whom she might need to call down the road on behalf of a client. For lawyers in regulatory practices, particularly in DC, access is important, and clients want a lawyer who can make a phone call knowing that the call will be returned.

"A midlevel associate," Rita continues, "ought to be using bar involvement to gain experience presenting on panels with other lawyers, getting her name out there, and developing a comfort level that she can either present on or moderate a panel." At this point, Rita recommends, the lawyer should have at least one article under her belt to help build her reputation in a more formalized manner.

As the lawyer becomes more senior, she needs to be more involved in client pitches and presentations. Rita recommends that associates approach partners and ask: "'Can I help you with that?'; even if you're not invited [to the pitch] at least you're helping in the preparation and [learning] the process. You're seeing how these things are put together."

Finally, it's very important for the "youngsters" to keep in touch with classmates. "You never know where your colleagues in law school are going to end up. Some of them are going to end up in companies that could be clients, so your electronic Rolodex is really important."

Rita recalls that no one ever taught her this. She slowly realized it over time, which made her think she was "behind the eight ball," but then notes that at one time or another, everyone worries about being in a difficult position or having to catch up.

Stumble On Your Clients

Once you've used your management-by-objective system and devoted 20 percent of your professional time to networking and building a name for yourself, how do you get clients? Rita says: "In the end, you stumble onto clients in the subway."

What she means is that the hiring of a particular lawyer often appears to be serendipitous. The lawyer was in the right place at the right time with the right reputation, precisely because the lawyer "managed herself by objective." She presented, participated on panels, wrote articles, and helped with client pitches. So yes, while it appears that you stumble upon clients, it's because you've done what was necessary to stay committed to your plan, which means "you do a lot of networking without necessarily any direct results, but with collective [results]."

Because you never know exactly how you will get a client, Rita emphasizes the importance of building relationships over time—networking on multiple levels to build the matrix. Don't forget about current clients, she cautions. Once a lawyer has a client, she needs to maintain and foster that relationship because the client may have more work for her lawyer and her colleagues. Moreover, every client is a source of referrals.

Confidence Drives Connections

Networking obviously pays off in terms of relationships and less obviously pays off in terms of the lawyer's ability to serve clients via the matrix of relationships that make up resources and necessary connections. What is perhaps even less obvious is that networking helps build the lawyer's confidence. And, importantly, clients are drawn to lawyers who are confident. Rita likens a lawyer's outward confidence to that of an actor onstage. "Consider everything from the way a lawyer walks into a room," she posits. "The lawyer's demeanor is important—her mannerisms, too. The lawyer must develop the ability to introduce herself to strangers and to overcome inhibitions with some degree of comfort. And, ultimately, she must stand on a podium and comfortably give a talk that is meaningful to the audience."

How did she build her confidence? Like Celia, Rita began using networking as a tool for career development before using it to develop business. She also started the traditional way by getting involved in the ABA Tax Section, gaining confidence by working on projects and making presentations. She learned to present and to moderate panels with challenging panelists. These are necessary skills for a lawyer to learn. Her recommendation is to "[learn to present and moderate panels] in a way that is most comfortable," she says, "and to be yourself. It's the only person you do well; anything else is an imitation."

"Part of being confident," Rita explains, "is being self-aware so you can learn from others. Thus, it's important to know your own skill set so that you can team with others to collectively "cover all the bases."

She jokes, "Every lawyer has limitations. You may even have to put five lawyers in a room to get 'the complete lawyer.'"

That is why, over time, Rita's networking strategy evolved as opportunities presented themselves through her partners. Working with other lawyers and particularly lawyers who bring a different skill set are important in a lawyer's business and professional development. In addition, a lawyer "gets more points internally" by working on a team rather than trying to develop business solo.

Rita also encourages others to learn from their experiences. The miserable experiences and the people who are very tough on you likely teach you more than the experiences that go well. Rita learned a lot about developing business by participating in pitches to clients. She also learned about what not to do. She comments that a lawyer "can step in it without even knowing." Her recommendation to younger lawyers: get involved in as many pitch teams as possible. "As a young lawyer . . . it's not necessary to sell yourself; you're selling your firm, you're selling your team, and you each bring something [different] to the table."

After Rita became a partner at Dewey Ballantine, she made the strategic decision to broaden both her experience and her network by joining the U.S. Treasury Department as the Associate Tax Legislative Counsel (TLC) in the Office of Tax Policy, where she was responsible for legislative and regulatory matters involving federal administrative and judicial tax procedure.

Rita remarks that her stint at the Treasury Department was confidence building because it was triage every day—"[You] either sink or swim," she says, dealing with Congress, dealing with the Treasury Department and the IRS, and dealing with the intra-agency chain of authority. She gained recognition often on very high-profile and somewhat controversial regulations. Rita's work as the associate TLC helped develop her network both at the IRS and in the private sector. She comments: "So that was just a different way . . . to network because I met a lot of people in the IRS [that] in a normal private-sector career I might not have known."

She also learned about how the IRS and Treasury operate from the inside rather than from the outside. The experience was a huge confidence builder and resulted in her achieving a higher profile in the community. For this reason, Rita recommends that young lawyers in a regulatory practice do a stint in government at the beginning or middle of their careers and then maintain the relationships. A lawyer needs to consider which government position makes the most sense given her career and networking objectives and then get the right government job.

Building Networks Outside the Law

Lawyers can build their practices by strategically building their networks outside of the law. Tax lawyers, for example, benefit from developing very good relationships with accounting firms. Accounting firms tend to have a foot in the door with companies because they provide audit services. And, because some tax lawyers move between accounting firms and law firms or have been in government and have transitioned to accounting firms, there tend to be significant cross-referrals.

Another way that Rita networked outside the profession was to present to the Tax Executives Institute (TEI), which was to company executives, not to colleagues at the bar. TEI is the premier organization for in-house tax professionals. After presenting, executives approached Rita with questions. She would then offer to come to the company, sometimes with a colleague, to talk to their staff "gratis." "It is a matrix; you have to make lots of different connections and think about how you can get in the door," she says.

Rita notes that like everyone, tax executives are busy and don't want a lawyer to waste their time. If, however, the lawyer has something to say that is of interest to their staff, they'll take a few free hours. In particular, companies are always looking for practical advice about what's going on within the IRS that is going to affect the way the company does business. They're looking for a lawyer who keeps up on changes in how the IRS is doing what it's doing. A tax lawyer could offer to talk to a tax department about current changes in IRS policy on summonses and what to do about them. Other examples include providing insight into how the IRS is conducting audits in the field as well as presentations on risk management. The latter presentations typically include ethics and are focused on the practicalities of managing a tax department's relationship with the IRS and avoiding mistakes that the government may take advantage of. This, she says, is "a different sort of networking." Like Celia, once Rita has invested the time in developing a presentation for TEI or another conference, she delivers a version of it to potential clients and other organizations.

Rita notes that, while far less direct, writing a treatise can help young lawyers develop their reputations. She and Jerry Kafka (her husband) wrote a premier treatise on litigating federal tax cases, *Litigation of Federal Civil Tax Controversies* (Kafka & Cavanaugh, *Litigation of Federal Civil Tax Controversies* [Thomson Reuters/Tax & Accounting] 2d Ed. 1997 & Supp. 2014-2). Whenever they wrote a supplement or addition, they sent complementary copies to clients and gave them to prospective clients when making an in-person presentation "so our names are up on their shelf."

Rita notes that companies can get overloaded with communications such as client alerts. On the other hand, if a lawyer writes an important article, she should carefully pick people to send it to. Another way for a lawyer to build her reputation is to write for the TEI newsletter, which lawyers at companies read. And, just about every tax lawyer, Rita says, reads *Tax Notes* or BNA Tax Management Portfolios, so they are also good places to publish.

Networking contributed to Rita's practice in other ways. Sometimes work comes in through colleagues, which is why networking with one's colleagues is important. For example, when the Affordable Care Act passed, one of the new taxes was a medical-device excise tax. Rita actually had experience with excise taxes in her prelaw life as an economist. Some of her nontax partners who had health care or deal practices had relationships with medical-device companies (or their parent company) and referred clients to her. They also referred trade associations of medical-device manufacturers. She advised the associations—helping their members navigate the various stages of Treasury regulations and their implications. This led to webinars for the associations, which led to more questions and interaction with potential clients.

Rita's Advice

Rita advises lawyers to build a reputation within their firms and in the community. While she wasn't always pitching, she knows these situations held potential for a client or professional connection. This holds true even for the connections made during pitches she didn't win. She advises lawyers to learn even from those experiences and focus on enlarging the circle of their networks. This, says Rita, will only increase a lawyer's chances of "stumbling onto new clients in the subway."

It can be hard because tax is a national practice. Geographically, Rita notes that she is located in DC, but there are many ways to make connections, and everybody knows everybody. It's six degrees of separation in the end. "So you just have to get out there and do it."

Rita continues, a lawyer wants "to get out there" in "whatever forms" she can. "People talk about playing golf—well, it does work. Not all of us want to go that route, but there are all sorts of ways to do it. Even think about your charitable activities; I'm on the board of an association, a nonprofit, and many of my partners are involved in nonprofit organizations around town and they're volunteers, they serve on boards, they serve on committees—you meet people that way too."

Rita advises junior partners to work with senior partners and to become part of the team that will be in place when the partner retires. While the client has to be sold on the team, inheriting clients is not impossible.

Rita says, "It isn't enough to be smart and capable; people must see it. A lawyer may have to get a bit out of her comfort zone to demonstrate her abilities. Part of this is not being afraid to ask questions. There is no such thing as a stupid question." Consequently, she says, "The task for us is to make sure that people understand and see what we bring to the table, and we shouldn't be shy about it."

This can be difficult, Rita admits, because partners are in the business of crafting the best work product possible. This means literally taking a red pen to associates' work product, which doesn't make the associates feel very good. To make matters worse, partners are not very good about acknowledging that the associate gave them a good work product to work with. Consequently, Rita says, "As I tell everybody, look in the mirror *every day* and remind yourself how terrific you are."

Rita's final advice: "Recognize that developing business takes time." She compares it to learning the craft of acting. "To be good, to be known, in either profession takes time, dedication, and practice. Yet somehow," she says, "there are some people who give the impression that lawyers should spring full-flown when they're born as potential partners in a law firm, but it doesn't work that way. It is a craft and there are tricks to it," she continues. "The same way actors have tricks. All of which can be learned through practice."

She says, "You're going to fall on your face sometimes. It's going to be gruesome. A lawyer will go home with her tail between her legs thinking, 'Oh, I just can't even face going back into the office tomorrow.' It's okay; everybody feels that way, and notice that you learned a lot. You won't make the same mistake twice."

Rita's Top 10 Networking Tips

1. Devote time to developing your business.
2. Network within your firm.
3. Especially as a younger lawyer, work with colleagues on business development.
4. If appropriate to your practice area, take a job that expands your network.
5. Don't expect any particular event to result in a new client. But remember: you will one day stumble onto clients in the subway.
6. Keep in touch with your network, especially law school classmates.
7. Get out there and present or speak on your subject matter.
8. Learn to present and moderate panels.
9. Be yourself.
10. It takes time—don't be deterred by failure, and learn from your mistakes.

Marianna Dyson
Partner, Miller & Chevalier, CHTD

Tax

Like a fine Kentucky bourbon. Sometimes your business strategy and networking strategy are like two sides of the same coin. Take Marianna Dyson, for instance: an early pioneer of "this quirky area of tax law" dealing with fringe benefits and the corresponding payroll tax and information reporting requirements. She and her former partner Handy Hevener figured out that their payroll tax niche was not only unique, but an entrée. Even the smart tax law professionals and their in-house departments don't spend much time developing this expertise or staying "tuned-up all the time" to answer the tough fringe benefit question. "So we really developed a model of being on the Rolodex for that oddball or difficult question," Marianna says.

The brash yet charming, whip-smart Kentucky native, like good bourbon, is an acquired and specialized taste. Many of her clients, smart tax lawyers or CFOs, tell her all the time that her expertise makes her the go-to person and a bargain, all at the same time. "You can hear them kind of doing a cost analysis. It's cheaper even at [Marianna's] hourly rate, they say, for us to call her and get it done and get it answered."

In other words, calling Marianna saves her clients money and gets them the all-important *right* answer quickly.

Marianna's networking strategy was to try to get her name on as many tax executives' Rolodexes as possible, even if just to be remembered as the lawyer with the funny accent who could answer oddball questions in her very specific area of the tax code—the theory being that her niche is the door opener. Then, if the question "blew up" into a bigger discussion around a controversy like an employment tax audit, she already had her firm's foot solidly inside the door. This strategy means that in some years Marianna may do several thousand dollars of business with a client and the next year a million dollars in work because "the thing really did blow up."

Consequently, Marianna focuses her networking on making herself known and available to the would-be buyers of her services, who are typically heads of large tax departments or corporate general counsels. She attends panels, gives speeches, and even goes to meetings where she thinks the "buyers" of her services will be. In this way, she can keep her network development hyperfocused.

Be the Hostess and Make It Fun

Marianna invests in her current network and current clients. In 2013, she hosted the First Annual Miller & Chevalier Dallas Tax Gals Dinner in Texas, where she does a lot of work. Although not a Texan, Marianna notes that being from Kentucky, "she talks more like them" than most and even lived in Texas as an army wife. She told her partners that she wanted to have a dinner in Texas to network with "all my buddies" and that it was "only going to be girls." Dallas has a plethora of women in tax department leadership roles, she points out.

In selling this to her partners, Marianna said, "[I knew] somebody was going to give me a project that will pay for all of this trouble, [while] continu[ing] the growth of our practice's reputation."

Marianna invited all of the women with whom she had worked for many years—and some of them brought other women from their departments. She invited 30, and 28 came. It was not overly expensive, and they had a "grand time." "Deep down," she added, "they're still just girls when it gets down to it."

She likes the dinner light, informal, and personal. She doesn't hire entertainment or provide speakers. "This year," she says, "we're going to look at the pictures of my daughter's wedding, and they'll enjoy that; they can entertain themselves." They are the entertainment. But in the end, Marianna makes her point perfectly clear. "I'm here to get work," she tells them to a chorus of knowing laughter. "So send work."

She admits that not everyone can pull that off, but it's part of her brand—straight talk with a sense of humor.

Hit the Wall? Call Marianna

For the most part, referrals from other professionals are unusual for Marianna. In fact, she can name the ten or twelve times she's had a referral, and those referrals have tended to come more from accounting firms, particularly when they have "hit the wall [in dealing with the IRS] on the controversy and are concerned they're not going to do well in appeals or they've got to get a case ready for litigation or to avoid litigation." In other words, the only time other tax professionals refer business to Marianna is when they recognize that they will likely lose the case for their client because they are so far out of their depth and need someone who knows this "quirky area of tax law."

If she gets the rare referral from a law firm, it's because they have a client conflict and can't take the case. Some lawyers, Marianna acknowledges, do very well networking with other lawyers in their practice area and have referrals to show for it. Members of the criminal bar are a good example, referring cases to one another all the time, she says. Because referrals are so scarce for her, she does not, as many others do, play a big role within bar associations.

Marianna remains focused on developing professional relationships with the tax professionals—the buyers of her services—who appreciate the value of her specialized legal counsel. One way she has extended and reinforced this strategy is to write for the publications her target audience reads, such as Tax Notes and the Tax Executives Institute publication. Another is to speak as often as she is invited to meetings and conferences sponsored by the Tax Executives Institute. These activities underscore her standing as a leader in this field.

Networking within an Organization

Given her focus on networking with the "buyers" of her services, Marianna networks with actual as well as potential clients. In this regard, she has found that it's "tricky" to network her services within a larger organization because it is often unclear who makes the final decision. It could be the vice president of tax, chief financial officer, or the general counsel positions. Consequently, her strategy is to build relationships within current clients and across their departments. In addition, she observes, "You have to remember that whomever you are working with may not be there indefinitely, so I'm always looking around for the succession plan within the client, and I develop—I try to develop—relationships with more than one person."

Consequently, Marianna takes advantage of situations where somebody young in the tax department is trying to learn something and comes to her for help. When that person asks her to review work to ensure he or she "described it right," she does so and often won't bill for it because, she says, "I want that person to look as good as he or she can and to get the credit."

Building relationships throughout a tax department doesn't always work, or at least, that strategy alone doesn't always work. Marianna represented a restaurant chain for more than 20 years, and when the new general counsel was hired from another firm, she simply decreed that her old firm would provide *all* legal services. Marianna had to work with her sources within the company—in this case, the head of the tax department—to make sure she would remain as outside counsel on payroll tax matters. Ultimately, the head of tax went to the CFO, who "trumped" the general counsel's decree.

Marianna's seen the decision-making authority shift over the last few years. When the Great Recession hit its stride and the economy tanked in 2007 and 2008, Marianna saw a change in how companies thought about tax services and shifted her networking accordingly. Companies tightened their belts and their budgets. For the first time, she saw a higher level of scrutiny with tax department budgets. Two groups within companies controlled these budgets: the general counsel and the tax departments. The general counsel would typically say to the tax departments, "Well, if you want a tax lawyer, I'll find you a tax lawyer, but it'll be a local tax lawyer at half the rate of someone from inside the [DC] Beltway."

The second shift Marianna observed was that companies adopted a competitive procurement process in which they started treating the lawyers like widgets. These changes "really compelled me to go back and work *almost conspiratorially* . . . with my contacts and with the heads of tax, to go in and try to interface and get to know the buyers, the ones who are actually controlling the budgets, very often in the general counsel's office."

In this way, the general counsels too could begin to see her value.

Marianna's shift in networking has also included heads of human resources, even though she had historically done very little work for them. This incongruity is because human resources is typically more focused on qualified plans, which are those retirement plans accorded favorable tax treatment. For advice on qualified plans, human resources departments usually rely upon consulting firms for advice. Notwithstanding, Marianna has had success. "Once the head of HR sees you . . . solve something that was driving them crazy, they get it that you understand this quirky little area."

Getting this work, however, has been "more of a crapshoot, and, frankly, more exhausting" for Marianna.

Marianna knows that her colleagues and friends at other firms know what she does and would refer her and her former partner, Handy. She says that comes from "kind of just from being around a long time." She doesn't have to stay top of mind with lunches, dinners, or drinks, but she does like to do them periodically, if for no other reason than to "visit" with a friend.

The Importance of a Personal Brand

Marianna advises younger lawyers—the "kids," as she calls them—to get out there and stake out what they do. Marianna observes that with lawyers who are most successful at branding, "there is something bigger about their personality." She is an example of that. The "bigger personalities" are more likely to be successful because they are less hesitant to say, "Look at me. I do this; I'm the one you want."

Marianna's strategy is a little different: She knows people tend to remember her as that "loud woman from Kentucky who's quick with a one-liner." She tells people, "Put my name in the Rolodex and next to it put *total fringe benefits, payroll taxes* and just keep me in the Rolodex or the contacts . . . and so that when you flip through when you have [a payroll tax] issue, [you'll remember] that sort of loud woman from Kentucky."

That is how Marianna has branded herself as *the* payroll tax person and uses her brand to make sure others understand who she is, what she does, and why she is the best choice.

Marianna's Advice

Pick up the phone. "Lawyers depend too much on voicemail and email." Marianna tells others: "Do not be afraid [to network], do not be afraid to ask for the work; the most powerful thing you have in networking is your index finger [to dial the phone], OK?"

Marianna most definitely uses her sense of humor to get more work, and that takes making a real live connection—not one through email. If she has a little free time, she will go through her contacts list and identify people she hasn't heard from, call them, and say something like, "'You've treated me shamefully. You haven't called, you haven't written,' and they start to laugh, and then about one in ten will say, 'I've got this issue, what can we do about this, can we talk about this?'"

Marianna says sometimes you have to call clients to remind them they need your services. You can't be afraid of interrupting them. She observes, "In other words, they're so overwhelmed they can't dial the phone, and I say to people that's what you have to do, you have to not be afraid . . . A lot of [in-house lawyers] don't mind being interrupted."

She knows her clients will call her when they "really put it in the ditch," but she likes to reach out to them and discuss more typical tax- and payroll-related engagements, too. It's a strategy she learned from her former partner, Handy. These are clients she's worked with for years, people who know and trust her. Marianna has been known to say something like "I have got to make that tuition payment to the University of Michigan. I need a project; what have you got?" She explains that people want to be remembered, and they like to laugh, which makes this approach unconventional but successful. Marianna is Southern, so she writes thank-you notes, pays attention to people's families, and asks about them. She also sends holiday and Christmas cards, even though it isn't "green."

Make It Easy for Your Clients

Marianna also advises lawyers to make it easy for prospective and actual clients to say "yes" to hiring or even just meeting with you. She says, "Don't push or prod them, but make them aware you're available to them should they need you."

For all of her directness, she actually prefers a less direct approach. One such strategy for getting a meeting is to call a client and say, "I know you get just inundated by people. I'd love to see you and catch up. I'll fit in any way I can, but please, please do not interrupt your life to see me. If I could swing by and just say 'hi,' that would be great."

Marianna has also gotten opportunities because she is patient, plays nicely with others, and, having practiced in Louisville, Kentucky, can appreciate being loyal to local counsel. Over many years, she regularly met with the tax department of a Midwestern company, during which she would share her expertise. On one such visit, the tax department—seeking advice but not wanting to jettison local counsel—finally decided it would be good to bring Marianna in for special projects, an arrangement in which everyone was a winner.

Marianna encourages people to persist and be thick-skinned. Just because prospects say "no" the first time, she has found that if they generally like the lawyer, it doesn't hurt to continue to build the relationship. If they are annoyed or won't take your call, move on. She knows there are definitely people out there who won't develop a taste for her style, or who don't think she's as smart as she should be to help, or knows that she came from a third-tier law school. That, Marianna says, is where being thick-skinned is really important. "It's like actors who tell you, you can't be thin-skinned, you're too short, you're too tall, you're too ugly, you're too blonde."

It's Like Fishing Lines

The best description Marianna has for networking is that it is "all about fishing lines." Imagine a fisherman who stands on the pier and starts throwing in lines, starting at one end of the pier and moving down to the other end of the pier. If the fisherman goes back to the very beginning to check the lines, he may have caught a fish. The key, she emphasizes, is that if the fisherman doesn't go back to check, he may miss that fish or fail to note success. "It's just a numbers game; you just sort of keep doing it," she says.

She believes that her firm, Miller & Chevalier, has done a good job of training clients to think of the firm as "one collective brain," which is the best way to deal with the competitive market. Thus, if one lawyer in the practice doesn't know something, another will. It helps to know one's own strengths and weaknesses and how to work with and involve other lawyers at one's firm.

Marianna used to give about 40 presentations, including webinars, annually. Along with these presentations, she created and shared outlines and other written materials. "Anything that gets written lives on."

In fact, Marianna recently got a big case from someone who tracked her down from an article she wrote for the Tax Executives Institute back in 2001. Somehow, the article got into the "broader space." This, she emphasizes, is more common than you might think. "I've had people chase me from law firm to law firm because of an outline I wrote in '99, so I am a big fan of trying to produce timely written pieces."

The other strategy that helped Marianna very early on, after she practiced about 15 years and had developed a solid reputation, was to field calls from reporters on fringe benefits and payroll tax issues. She made her intention clear: "Rule number one, [she says to reporters,] I care less about being quoted in this article than my helping you get it right, getting the understanding of the law and the background."

As a consequence, she's been quoted numerous times by the Associated Press, Reuters, the *Wall Street Journal*, and *Forbes*. She guesses correctly that reporters keep lists of people who are willing to help them and provide verifiable information on background in a neutral manner. Marianna even offers to read the reporters' descriptions of the law to ensure they get it right.

Marianna's Top 10 Tips

1. Specialize and become known for your niche.
2. Be a bargain at twice your hourly rate—in other words, offer great value and insight.
3. Be a resource and build the relationship.
4. Remember people and their families—send cards.
5. Be a host, be fun.
6. Write.
7. Have a sense of humor and use it.
8. Pick up the phone.
9. Check your "fishing lines."
10. Sell "the brain trust"—be known for providing the pathway to any question in your firm's practice area.

Conclusion

These inspiring women are very different and so network very differently. Yet they share common themes. They each make time to network and are intentional about their networking. They deliberately devote their precious time to maximize the benefit. Not one of these women networks haphazardly or just when she has time.

These women are patient. Their expectations are reasonable and in line with reality. Their focus and energy is on building a name for themselves, and they have succeeded as a result of the totality of their actions. You can do this, each said, by being intentional, strategic, and dedicated. Maintain an empowering mindset and focus on the long game. What you do now may or may not have immediate results. It doesn't matter. But if you have a strategy, what you do now is an investment in your future and will pay off.

Chapter 3

Social Media

Dee A. Schiavelli

Social media is a relatively new way of communicating on the Internet. Starting as a college networking idea, it has grown into a major networking and communication force. "Social media are computer-mediated tools that allow people to create, share or exchange information, ideas, and pictures/videos in virtual communities and networks," describes Wikipedia. Do not mistake social media as a fad: it is how people are communicating in today's world on all levels—personal and business. Because it is driven by technology, it will continue to evolve and change, but is unlikely to disappear.

The HistoryList (a Web-based platform used by history-related organizations) recently said, "Of the greatest inventions in the last 1000 years the Printing Press was considered #1." Why? Because it allowed literacy to expand. The printing press enabled people to communicate, to share, to learn. Social media is a similar example of significant change in the 21st century that also allows people to communicate, to share, to learn.

Why Should Lawyers Use it?

The Internet and social media have permanently altered the way clients evaluate their need for legal services. Today's prospective clients actively seek out information for themselves, find lawyers through Internet searches, and arrive at decisions about their legal needs, often before they retain a lawyer. By the time a lawyer is contacted, the prospect has already vetted choices. Social media is not the goal in and of itself, but by participating in it, you can achieve your goals.

What Platforms Are There?

There are many social media platforms to choose from. Currently, the most popular among lawyers are LinkedIn, Facebook, Twitter, and blogs. But, Google+, Pinterest, and YouTube are growing in popularity among lawyers as people learn how to best use them.

in LinkedIn provides a professional network among businesspeople (although it is not exclusive to them), tracks careers and business relationships, and focuses on each individual's experience. A lawyer's LinkedIn profile should clearly indicate the value the lawyer offers, not just the features of her practice. The LinkedIn summary should speak more about what the client receives. This space is an opportunity to include industries served, type of clients, examples of matters, how the lawyer works with clients, and so on. Include practice, of course, but talk about client expectations too.

f Facebook is more social and includes activities of its members within their individual networks. It allows photos posted by the owner of the account but can include those posted by others. Friends share information with friends. It has a business side in its Pages section, and many lawyers are using Pages to promote their practice and gain a following.

t Twitter provides a platform for short communications, allowing people to share information as it is happening with those following them. It has grown more sophisticated than its origins. Today's Twitter reports people's experiences at the moment. News is often tweeted when it happens anywhere. A revolution can be sent around the world instantly by someone who is there to see it. Information from a conference is shared with followers while the speaker is still onstage. Everything can be tweeted as it occurs, whether it is bad behavior or a new product. Lawyers who use Twitter often alert followers to new law, share their blogs, or give notice about new activities.

g+ Google+ focuses on creating a network identified by categories (circles) and allows the user to communicate and share information within them. Circles might be business colleagues, clients, family, and so on. The user assigns contacts to her circles and chooses a circle of the network to share information with.

A blog (short for *weblog*) is a website where people post articles. People can subscribe to the blog, or the author can send it out via email to people he or she knows. Initially, blogs need to be promoted, but they can also be linked from websites, LinkedIn, and Facebook for readers to find. They also are found through Internet searches on topics. Blogs are very popular in that they are topic oriented. For lawyers, the best blogs are sent weekly, but more often than not, their blogs are monthly. Key benefits of a blog are that they can open communication between the blogger and the reader, educate, and share ideas.

Pinterest focuses on pictures and visual communication and is best used for creating interest in the message. Few lawyers are using Pinterest yet, but it is relatively new.

Each of these social media platforms differs significantly from the others, but all offer lawyers various ways to communicate with their network and with others seeking to find them.

Who's Using it?

- According to LexBlog, since 2006, there has been a 356 percent increase in social media use. (LexBlog, 2013)
- As of 2013, 2.27 billion people are online. (United Nations)
- Ninety-one percent of online adults use social media regularly. (GrabStats)
- The 2013 *In-house Counsel New Media Engagement Survey* said, "LinkedIn is the social media source in-house counsel uses most to obtain information and expand their contacts."
- As of January 2014, LinkedIn counts over 700,000 LinkedIn profiles in the legal industry. (LinkedIn 2014)
- Seventy-six percent of consumers go online to find a lawyer. (Lawyers.com, 2012)
- According to the ABA's *2014 Legal Technology Survey Report*, 90 percent of lawyers said their firms are on LinkedIn and 52 percent are on Facebook.

Which Platforms Are Best for Lawyers?

Most professionals believe that LinkedIn is hands down the best for lawyers. It's more focused on business and more professional in its approach. No one can post anything on your profile, communication within your network is private, and it has many ways to connect and share information. The platform continues to improve, adding new ways for users to demonstrate and share information that sets them apart from others in their field. Blogging, though, has drawn in more business because it can educate a prospect more quickly and adds obvious value to followers. "Blogging will remain the #1 way to generate new business because it creates great content on a regular basis; driving traffic back to your site is going to remain the #1 way to generate new leads," says Stephanie Fasco of Convert with Content.

All social media platforms should be explored to see which ones are best for you and your firm. Anyone can use social media to develop her practice, even as a novice. It will give more visibility than could be achieved without it and help users to be found. Social media also builds valuable relationships with people who can use or refer one's services that would otherwise remain unknown.

The following interviews are with women lawyers who have successfully used some aspects of social media to bring in new business. Their stories will tell you how you can, too.

Tracy Krall

Managing Attorney, Krall Law Office PLLC
Family Law

Social Media: LinkedIn, Facebook

Tracy Krall is a solo practitioner who first started using social media in 2011 when she opened her practice in family law. Coming from a larger firm, she thought it was important to use LinkedIn as a way to develop her own practice. Tracy says, "I have a Facebook business account, but mostly I use LinkedIn." It's good to keep a presence on Facebook because you never know where new business will come from and Facebook often has a different audience from LinkedIn. If you add information to LinkedIn, though, you can just as easily add it to Facebook and tweet it at the same time.

Tracy's practice in family law focuses on divorce and the many sensitive issues families experience, from custody matters to parental relocation. Her goal is to project that sensitivity in her website and on her social media platforms.

When Tracy started her practice, she did not know much about how to use LinkedIn. Although she had an account from her prior law firm, her profile was pretty bare. Being with a large firm, she relied upon the partners to bring in work. All lawyers should maximize their LinkedIn profile regardless of whether they are with a small or large firm or are a new lawyer or skilled. It should be a work in progress, changing as they grow in experience.

Once out on her own, Tracy realized she needed help and took a webinar offered by the State Bar of Arizona on how to set up a profile on LinkedIn. The webinar was very helpful but made her realize she needed more personal training. "I followed up and got a private coaching lesson on the ins and outs of LinkedIn. I was then able to do a really good profile, which I believe sets me apart from other LinkedIn profiles where they are basically reciting their resumes."

What Tracy did with her profile was to tell a story—not about all she could do for clients, but a personal story of one client. Through the story, Tracy presented how she treated and worked with clients along with demonstrating her skills as a lawyer. Many lawyers write their profiles as a CV or resume focusing on the features they provide, not the benefits or value that clients receive.

"I'm far from being able to say I am a connoisseur of using LinkedIn. I'm not as proactive as I should be; I'm not technologically savvy. But I wanted to at least have my profile primed and ready to go so that it is out there and accessible."

Creating a profile is only the first step in using LinkedIn. Since Tracy created hers, LinkedIn has made many improvements to the profile platform, so there is much more that a lawyer can add based on her experience and activity. For example, articles, videos, slideshows, and more can be added to a lawyer's summary section, along with announcements of upcoming events such as speaking engagements. Anything the lawyer publishes can be added to the publishing section of her profile. These are new features since Tracy first set her profile up, and they help establish and build a lawyer's reputation in her area of law.

The fear of technology can keep many lawyers from using social media. They often don't find the time to learn how to use new platforms, update them, or keep up with advances. Another obstacle that holds some lawyers back from effectively using social media is a lack of time to participate. Many who have ventured forth have created their basic profile, but it often lacks substance. Having a basic profile is a good first step, but it may not communicate what a prospect is looking for.

Clients that have come to Tracy through social media have first seen her website or an email (where she has her LinkedIn link) or were given a referral. Tracy explains, "I learned from the webinar to add my LinkedIn address to my email signature. I've been doing that, and some people see the link and go to it."

That is how Tracy got one of her clients. Her client found her through a slightly convoluted trail that led to Tracy's LinkedIn profile. Before the client had chosen representation, she was served divorce papers by her husband's lawyer, and she saw the lawyer had a LinkedIn profile. This led the woman to search LinkedIn for her own attorney. Once she saw Tracy's profile, she thought Tracy was very warm and compassionate, that she was more caring and friendlier than other attorneys out there, and that was why she decided to go with her.

One of the easiest ways to share your LinkedIn profile is to add it to your email signature. People are more likely to click on that link to learn more about you personally because the link is conveniently there. You can also easily add the link to your website.

Tracy says, "I got a referral from an attorney that I met on LinkedIn. We found each other there and connected. Later we met for coffee and he had a referral for me. The only way I knew him was through LinkedIn."

Many lawyers who are looking for opportunities to give and get referrals use LinkedIn to find compatible practices and experience. LinkedIn is one of the easiest places to look. Through the advanced search feature, you can tailor your research.

For Tracy, "I got more business from LinkedIn about a year into using it. My client emailed me through my website, and when she came in to meet with me, she was filling in the section on my intake sheet that asked 'How did you hear about us?' She checked off LinkedIn."

The first step in maximizing LinkedIn is to recognize its value and then learn how to capitalize on it. Tracy feels that if she sets aside 15 minutes in the morning to look around her account, she will find ways to connect with her network.

Tracy advises other lawyers to use social media to build their practice. It's free. She has a very small marketing budget. "Social media was very helpful when opening a new firm and has helped me to create greater visibility and develop a reputation." And it continues to be valuable to those lawyers that have invested the time to learn how to best use it.

In the past, it took lawyers years to build their reputation, but today with social media you can build your reputation more quickly at an earlier stage in your career. The more you do and the more you share, the greater your reputation becomes. Learn to strategically use LinkedIn. Share information with clients, prospects, and referral sources that is interesting and/or valuable to them. Do this judiciously and stay top of mind. This will add value to your relationship.

Ruth Carter

Managing Attorney, Carter Law Firm

Intellectual Property, Social Media, Business and Internet Law, Business Formation and Contracts, Flash Mob Law

Social Media: Blog (Firm and Personal), Facebook, Google+, LinkedIn, Twitter, YouTube

Ruth Carter, a solo practitioner, first started using social media in law school before she opened her practice. She intuitively knew she needed a strong network before she even graduated and built one among other law students and movers and shakers in the legal industry, seeking out lawyers with whom she wanted to connect. Ruth also kept her "ear to the ground" for issues facing future clients. By the time she passed the bar, she had a substantial network and a lot to share with a potential readership.

"When I opened my practice, I said I'm not putting any money into marketing until we create my website. I opened my practice with marketing through social media right away. I spend about 50 percent of my time, including networking, on marketing. I think when you are a solo it's par for the course; you are not only practicing law but running a business."

Ruth uses almost all the major social media platforms. She's active on Twitter and has a YouTube channel for the law firm, a firm Facebook page, and a blog specifically for her practice, Carter Law Firm. She also has a personal blog, *The Undeniable Ruth*, and writes for the blog *Attorney at Work*. She's an active participant on LinkedIn and on Google+.

Ruth can say with confidence that she gets new business because she is using social media. At least once a week she gets emails from people who say, "I saw your blog about X. Can I talk to you about my problem?"

Blogging is significant to Ruth. While she blogs regularly, her posts are typically written outside the nine-to-five work hours. She releases a new post on her personal blog every Tuesday, on her law firm blog weekly, and on *Attorney at Work* once a month. She also records on the firm's YouTube channel, *Ruth Carter YouTube*, every Wednesday.

It is sometimes difficult to quantify if new business comes from social media activities or another source. Ruth realizes, though, that social media is all about relationships. "Through social media, I am creating and maintaining relationships that are leading to referrals. Probably 50 percent of my new business comes from Internet searches, which is often because they found a blog post on a topic related to their problem." It is clear that her active involvement in social media creates a more robust presence for her in Internet searches, and that has helped generate new business.

Ruth puts out a video from her office every week on YouTube, recording topics that she thinks would be relevant to prospects. Occasionally she goes on Facebook or LinkedIn and asks, "'Does anyone have a topic they would like me to tackle on my weekly video?' Sometimes that is where I get my topics." In addition, she keeps on top of relevant subjects in the news, and sometimes her contacts send her a request saying, "You should do a post about this."

Building a social media network does not happen the moment you decide to use it. In Ruth's situation, it started early while she was in law school. Since she had already built up a decent network leading up to and through law school, when she launched new media channels, it was easy to reach out to her existing network and get attention. "I'm a big believer in the idea that social media is a communications tool for interacting with others. Social media is not a digital billboard. It's about creating and maintaining relationships with others through dialogue.

Ruth says, "On Facebook, the law firm has 365 likes; I have 1,284 Twitter followers for the firm, 7,129 views on my YouTube channel, and on LinkedIn I have over 1,000 network connections. As of today, I have had 117,612 hits on my website—over 84,000 for this year [2014] alone.

"Social media is not a digital billboard."

"One of my blog posts got a lot of attention on Reddit this year, so 33,000 of those hits came from that in one day. It crashed my site."

Reddit.com is an information link site, and there are Reddits for just about every topic you can think of, including some for lawyers. Some topics are more popular than others. One of the very popular ones is titled "Today I Learned," and people post links to things that are fun facts. "Someone did a 'Today I Learned' post about a blog post I did looking at the trademarks between two companies, and it was extremely popular. It got over 40,000 hits in the course of three days."

Ruth's knowledge of technology helps her to be fearless. One of the benefits of having a blog as a law student is that she accomplished the blog and website learning curve early, which helped her when creating a website for the law firm. She learned how to do tech things, which became handy when she created her own site. Ruth says she can handle most things on the back end.

Many lawyers are focused on return on investment (ROI), invest in various social media platforms, and want to quantify how much business will come from their social media efforts. Ruth learned to let all of that go. She says: "These are tools. There are no guarantees. You get out what you put into it." Ruth does not look at social media in terms of how much business it will directly generate. She looks at it as "this is how I maintain relationships with people."

Using social media for Ruth is all about attitude—it's a mindset. Look at Twitter. Ruth does not watch TV news at night because she follows news outlets on Twitter. Ruth uses Twitter to follow national and international news organizations that are important to her, her friends, professional contacts, and people she wants to have as professional contacts. One of the best ways Ruth knows of to break the ice is to engage with someone on Twitter.

Ruth says if there is someone you want to know, all you have to do is start following them on Twitter, keep an eye on what they post, and wait for an opportunity to respond to a tweet that is relevant to why you want to be connected to them. Or, if they have done something worthy of praise, you can probably praise them on Twitter and they will see that and likely appreciate it. And if they say, "I'm going to be at this conference," you can respond, "I look forward to meeting you there."

Ruth has a great Twitter story. "When I was a law student, the school career center brought in a panel of lawyers that were doing things that were different. One of the people on the panel was Sam Glover, who owns and writes the Lawyerist.com. I didn't know him at the time, but he's a lawyer, blogger, a cool guy, and I determined that he needed to be my new best friend. I had a laptop with me, so I immediately jumped on Facebook, LinkedIn, and Twitter to find his online presence. By the time he finished doing his pitch about *Law-yerist*, I liked his blog on Facebook, was following him on Twitter, and tweeted out about how cool it was that I was sitting here where he was speaking at my law school.

"When he sat down, he got his phone out and started looking at it while the rest of the panel was speaking. I could tell the moment he saw the email that told him someone at the event just tweeted about him. He smiled and I saw his eyes start scanning the room. I use the same photo on all social media, so I am always identifiable. After the event was over and all the speakers were hanging out so we could chat with them, I joined his conversation and he just stopped and said 'Oh, you're Ruth.' Ice broken. We have been friends to this day."

"I have had a lovely back-and-forth Twitter exchange with people for over a year now—long before I met them. With Twitter, it is easy to reach out to people in a natural conversational way."

People do not think that this type of thing happens, but it does if you use it. Ruth says, "Using your social media tools is key. If you don't use them, you don't benefit. It's not enough to be just out there. You have to let people know. Don't be afraid of it. Learn how to use it—put in the effort."

Obviously, Ruth is going to continue to use social media. She is one of the lawyers who will be open to trying new things as they come along, and she thinks others should be, too. Her main advice to any-one who is thinking about using social media for marketing is to "real-ize that social media is a communication tool. It is about interacting and relationships. Don't treat it like a billboard." She recommends "talking with people, not at them." Ruth has cultivated an approach-able presence through her use of social media and her blog. Even if you are not as laid-back and casual as Ruth, you can still let your personality come through.

Ruth follows these social media rules:

1. Don't put anything online that you wouldn't put on the front page of the newspaper.
2. Assume everything that you post will be seen by four people: your best friend, your worst enemy, your boss, and your mother. If you are not OK with one of those people seeing it, don't put it out there.

Melissa Duncan
Partner, Duncan Law PLLC
Bankruptcy Law
Social Media: YouTube, Blog, Facebook, Google+, Twitter, LinkedIn

Melissa Duncan practices law with her husband and father-in-law in North Carolina. She and her husband, Damon, made a conscious decision to use social media in lieu of print advertising to build their bankruptcy practice. In four years, they have built a substantial practice primarily through this strategy.

"We started using social media when we came out of law school and took the bar. We knew we would join the family firm but didn't want to jump into the same legal family law market of Charlotte, which is where my father-in-law, Terry Duncan [the founding partner], practices. We started our bankruptcy practice in Greensboro."

Melissa and Damon have been using social media instead of traditional advertising for over a year now in an effort to save money and promote their practice. They felt this was the most cost-effective way to build a reputation. One of the first things they did was to create *Duncan Law Blog* to push information out. They did use one area of advertising by using pay per click and search engine optimization (SEO) of their website. Their ROI was more than the cost of the advertising. "Pay per click is an Internet advertising model used to direct traffic to websites in which advertisers pay the publisher (typically a website owner) when the ad is clicked," according to Wikipedia.

Almost everything we do is online, although occasionally we send out a letter targeted to a certain group of people. We realized that if we needed a dentist or doctor, we went online (after we got referrals) to see what the reviews were, how they communicated, and if they were relevant to us.

> *"Almost everything we do is online. . ."*

We wanted to be relevant to people who went online looking for attorneys, so it was important for us to have social media accounts, not only to get clients but also to build relationships with other attorneys."

Melissa says they established their social media accounts prior to graduating law school. Of course they could not hold themselves out as lawyers, but they started networking with attorneys, especially attorneys in different practice areas. They wanted to build relationships before they were practicing. Then, once they started practicing, they already had a foundation for referrals online.

"We use LinkedIn, Facebook, Twitter, YouTube, Google+, and the blog. I belong to some groups on LinkedIn. One is a national bankruptcy group; others are more local affiliations. We've created our personal profiles and our firm profile on Google+. We really like Google+." The Duncan Law LLP Google+ platform focuses entirely on the practice areas of all three partners. It includes photos, posts, videos, and client reviews, giving them a five-star ranking from reviewers. Mostly they address questions people ask in both their posts and in their videos.

YouTube has been their most powerful social media tool, where they have built their reputation and established creditability through a series of videos on frequently asked bankruptcy questions. The You-Tube videos also feed the blog content. Melissa says they knew that the YouTube videos were working to generate business when they begin to have client intake forms that indicated the referral source had been television commercials although the firm had never used that medium. Clients believed they had seen them on television even though the firm has only used YouTube.

More and more lawyers are experimenting with videos. Some are quite good and professionally done, but too many focus on the lawyer, not on their clients' needs. One of the key things to remember about social media is that it is not about the lawyer, but about the people who are looking for a lawyer. It's about their issues, their needs, and resolving their problems.

Melissa and Damon's goal is to be known as the authority on bankruptcy law in their region. Melissa's social media strengths are in YouTube, blogging, and Twitter. The firm features their blog on their website, and they write posts regularly. Once something is posted on their website, Melissa and Damon promote it on all other social media platforms. Melissa says their friends on Facebook think of them as "the bankruptcy attorneys."

"We send our blog posts to just about everyone. We wrote regularly, so we put quite a bit of information out before our baby was born. We were blogging three times a week, posting Monday, Wednesday, and Friday. Our goal is to be consistent and frequent enough so people know when to expect new content."

Their blogs are either articles or specifically address questions people have asked, but Twitter is the platform geared to responses.

Melissa says Twitter should be 90 percent responses. It should be a dialogue, not a monologue. Other social media platforms are a monologue, such as LinkedIn, Facebook, and videos.

"When we first started practicing in the fall of 2009, we attended a local event with some attorneys. I met one lawyer from an adjacent town who said, 'Hi, I'm so and so.' We had connected on Twitter. I recognized his face because we were tweeting back and forth. I remember thinking, 'The online networking is working.' I remember leaving the conversation feeling confident that if he ever has someone who needs bankruptcy law legal services, he will contact us. And I knew him solely from Twitter."

To develop content, Melissa says they base it on questions people are asking them and then turn those into a blog post. "Actually, that is the hardest part about it. We're always meeting with new clients, and when they ask us questions, we think, 'Do we have an article about that on our blog?' and if not, we make a note. We maintain a spreadsheet to track what we have written about, and if we haven't addressed an issue, we write a blog post about it."

It helps that Melissa and Damon are in agreement. It can be difficult if only one person wants to write the blog. It does require a lot of dedication and organization to maintain it. "We have to be sure we are on the same page and have the same goals because it is easy to say, 'Well, I'm not going to deal with it this week; I'll do it next week,' and then next week it doesn't get done."

Melissa's father-in-law, also a lawyer with the firm, writes articles but doesn't blog. He doesn't use Facebook or Twitter or other social media platforms, but he has made quite a number of videos that are on their website.

In fact, each of the three partners has done a lot of YouTube videos that can all be accessed from their website under different practice areas. They also have linked them to Google+ but not to LinkedIn and Facebook, which they could do. They predominantly use the videos to educate their audience on each area of practice.

Melissa says that in a small firm the time allocated to maintaining social media needs to be shared equally among the partners. This ensures that everybody is aware of what is being posted and agrees on the goals. Like all marketing activities, having a strategy is important, but often lawyers don't—they just dive in. In Melissa's firm, she says it has been more evolution than strategy.

They have continued to pursue their ultimate goal—to use social media to build their business. "We are aware of what the social media platforms are and know how to use them. What we are always asking is, 'What is the next big thing?' because social media is not stagnant. There will be new social media platforms. It's just a matter of keeping your eyes and ears open to be aware of the next platform. But we'll never drop our current social media platforms."

She adds, "Even large firms can benefit from using social media. It's not just for small firms. We look at it this way—the Fortune 50 is on LinkedIn. And it's free."

Melissa has been using social media for over four years. Like many lawyers, some of the frustrations she's experienced are in measuring ROI. "I can't always see exactly if people are finding me from my account on Twitter or from a referral from a friend on Facebook who reads a blog post. You sometimes feel that you are putting all this out there and working hard to get on social media platforms, but it can be hard to measure your success. You ask, 'Is it really working?' but then we look back over the past four years and we've built a successful business."

Since law school, Melissa and Damon have been able to build a reputation in Greensboro among other lawyers. They try to connect with new people; established attorneys whom they didn't meet in school refer clients to them. Melissa says, "That says a lot—we made a connection and we made the relationship strong enough to have them refer clients to us." It has only been four years, and people did not really know them before. That shows they are doing a good job building relationships—they see that people are coming to them because of the connections they made on social media.

One of the biggest fears lawyers have is that social media will take an enormous amount of time. Melissa realizes that is a possibility, so she approaches it with dedication and balance. Right now they spend a couple of hours a week on social media activities. They try to stay on top of it by dividing the work between her and Damon.

Melissa's advice to other lawyers regarding using social media is that it is a place to put themselves out there on a wide variety of platforms.

> "One very important aspect of social media is the ability to build relationships with other lawyers and to get and give referrals through those networks."

Lawyers should look for like-minded people that they can build relationships with. "It's hard to go wrong using social media. I think it is a really, really great thing. You can start a relationship anywhere without doing it in person. You can always benefit by using it."

Once you have established a relationship through social media, it can lead to a personal friendship as well as a good business relationship.

Catherine Tucker

Managing Attorney, Law Office
of Catherine Tucker

Reproductive Law

Social Media: Blog, Facebook, LinkedIn, Pinterest, Twitter

Catherine Tucker is a solo practitioner who initially started practicing law as an assistant district attorney in Massachusetts and later with the New Hampshire Department of Justice. She first began using social media when she started her reproductive law practice.

Catherine has always been open to marketing and uses a few different social media platforms to support her efforts. "Marketing is a pretty substantial part of what I do. My practice as a whole is based on education and marketing combined. There is a lot of overlap between those two areas."

Catherine spends at least 15 hours a week on social media educating people through speaking and writing, including through her blog, which is found on her website, Law Office of Catherine Tucker, www.tuckerlegal.com. As her practice is somewhat unique, she feels that it is a good way to educate people who are directly impacted by infertility or others who need some education about infertility as it impacts their family members.

Catherine says it is easy to be found through the Internet. Everybody Googles. They look for friends and colleagues, professionals to do business with, things to buy, and places to go. People also Google to solve problems, whether it is trying to understand what a doctor has said or finding a lawyer who fits particular needs. That is why Catherine is using social media. "I've tried to tailor some of my information so that it is available either directly through Google or by coming to my site through other links."

Catherine wants to harness the wealth of information that is out there for everyone and help people, especially those talking about infertility. She says surrogacy in particular is an area where there is a lot of misinformation. For example, if you Google *surrogacy* in New Hampshire, you will find only information about what is allowed in New Hampshire. And if you are a same-sex couple, you will find that it is not allowed in New Hampshire, along with other things that are misleading. Catherine practices both in New Hampshire and Massachusetts, and their laws are vastly different in the area of surrogacy.

"One of the things I'm trying to address is the myths surrounding the law so that people can get accurate information based on their situation. That's why you are hiring an attorney, because if you just want to read the law, you can, but if you want someone to interpret the law, that's different. If you want to have the law work for your situation, it helps to have an attorney working with you to help you sort through what the law says versus what it means. Something that I constantly come across is that people think same-sex couples can't use surrogates in New Hampshire. I try to tailor a lot of my education to address the myths that I hear."

Catherine is using a variety of social media platforms because each serves a different purpose. She uses her blog to write articles and educate. She uses LinkedIn and Facebook for building networks and sharing information. She uses Twitter to communicate. And she uses Pinterest (Law Office of Catherine Tucker) to engage people who are experiencing infertility issues. Tracking whether business comes from these sites is more diffi-

> *"In retrospect, I probably should have had a strategy. I would have saved myself a lot of time."*

cult. "In retrospect, I probably should have had a strategy. I would have saved myself a lot of time. I would have had a plan for what I was going to do and set out how much time I was going to spend on a task each week. I think that looking back on things, that it would have been a better overall plan for building my practice. But I just did things as I thought of them."

Catherine does not say she gets business directly from social media, but people who get her name from another channel are going to Google her and then they are going to come across her social media sites and learn more about her practice. The Pinterest site especially gives them a more personal focus of her practice. She posts cartoons as well as serious information on it. People can look and find some comfort there, see that she understands what they are going through, that she supports them and wants to provide them with information as well as the materials that may make their journey a little bit easier.

Looking through everything Catherine has put on her Pinterest page, you get a sense of what it would be like if you were seeking a lawyer practicing infertility law and found this page. You would feel comfortable and comforted and not alone. You would feel that someone actually understood. Some of the posts are funny, and others are serious, addressing fears or difficulties that people have. That is often hard for lawyers to portray. You can see how people would view her Pinterest site and her blog and feel good, believe that she knows the legal issues, that she understands their problem, and that she can address their fears and concerns.

Catherine says that was her goal. She wanted to educate people, not just clients and potential clients going through the issues she addresses, but also to help their family members understand. Educating others can make a big difference in the way people are treated and ultimately in the way that the public reacts. She wants to spread awareness because that will help the infertility community as a whole—her clients as well as all the other people going through treatments.

Catherine is not the only lawyer with a Pinterest site, but she seems to be one of the few using it effectively. "Lawyers write a lot and read a lot, and what we write is really long. A client can get caught up in all these words, so the ability to look at things from a visual perspective can make it easier to understand and can be nice for people."

The saying goes, "A picture is worth a thousand words." If you can put into a picture what you are saying, it helps people to connect with you and see that you understand. That's what Catherine's Pinterest site does. It is a picture of what people are concerned about; it shows understanding and offers ideas and suggestions.

Catherine feels that if she had not been using social media, her practice might not be where it is today. "My ultimate goal as an advocate for those struggling with infertility is to be able to spread the word to the community in general. I'm very happy that I began to pursue this goal. I've put in substantial time for the articles that I've written and the Pinterest site I've put together. But it's absolutely been worth it."

Many lawyers feel Pinterest wouldn't work in their area of law. Catherine disagrees. She thinks you just need to do some thinking about it. Don't create a Pinterest site that is basically screen shots of things off your website. "You want to focus on the visual nature of Pinterest. If a potential client visits your Pinterest site, what is going to draw them in to spend a little time looking at it for entertainment purposes? In every area of law, there is going to be something. Whether it's tax law or criminal defense, there's going to be visuals available. You can use the linking features to add things from other sites to yours. It is a sharing platform. You share with others, they share with you. You may unearth some unexpected clients that will find their way to you."

Catherine says lawyers should not be afraid to create their own visuals. "As lawyers, we need to break out of the mold of only reading and writing. Think about pictures. As a trial lawyer, I am always thinking about how I can sell my concepts to a jury. Pictures work when explaining really complicated things to a jury in the most basic terms so they can understand." What pictures would you use to explain something to a jury? Translate those to your Pinterest site and explain those same concepts to the general public.

Catherine's advice for other women lawyers is to "just do it. Use social media. Try it out. If you don't like it, you can take it down. It's not a significant financial investment, assuming you are doing the work yourself. So, go ahead and try new things and see how they work."

Nicole Black

Lawyer, Author, Director of Business Development and Community Relations at MyCase, Of Counsel, Fiandach & Fiandach

Civil Litigation and Criminal Defense

Social Media: Blog, Facebook, Google+, LinkedIn, Twitter

Niki Black has practiced law in upstate New York since 1996. Niki has used many social media vehicles to create a career that she feels passionate about. She is also featured in chapter 5, Writing. This interview focuses on Niki's other social media outlets, which include Facebook, Google+, LinkedIn, and Twitter.

Niki is a good example of a woman who is an "out-of-the-box" thinker, who built her law practice and then successfully moved on to a law-related business using social media. She demonstrates how you can find business and opportunities through social media.

Niki initially created multiple blogs. Around that same time, Facebook started up in universities, but only college students could get an account. Niki picked up on its possibilities and realized that it too might have great potential for her practice. "In 2007, just before Facebook opened up to the public, I went to my college and joined it with an .edu address. Now I had a Facebook account, but there were very few lawyers on Facebook. So I created a Facebook group called Lonely Lawyers on Facebook."

Shortly after Facebook opened to the public, Twitter appeared. Niki was not interested in Twitter until she read a blog by Kevin O'Keefe of LexBlog on why lawyers should be on Twitter. "There weren't too many lawyers on Twitter, but I joined around 2007/2008. The rest is history. I'm now one of the most followed lawyers by legal professionals on Twitter."

Some of her accolades include:

1. One of *Six Savvy Law & Technology Resources* (*Forbes* blog)
2. Winner of the 2008 Shorty Award honoring the best legal Twitter
3. #3 (out of 736) on the *JD Supra Blog: Lawyers to Follow on Twitter*
4. #5 on *Online Cases Blog: Top 100 Twitterers in the Legal World*
5. #40 on Top 100 Twitter Feeds for Law Students (OnlineBest Colleges.com)
6. One of the Top 50 Twitter Feeds for Paralegals
7. One of the Most Followed Twitterers on Twitter (Knowledge Management)
8. One of the 50 Lawyers and Legal Professionals You Should Follow (Top Lawyer Coach)
9. One of the 15 "Must" Follow Law-Related Twitter Feeds (Rick Glaser, Wells & Drew)
10. One of the Top 50 Lawyers to Follow on Twitter (Klout)

Niki has become renowned for her Twitter feeds. She maintains three Twitter accounts. On @lawtechtalk, she follows and discusses technology as it applies to lawyers and the practice of law, and she is considered one of the top technology curators on Twitter by Top 10 Twitter Lists for Techies. She has over 2,700,700 followers to date.

Niki's second Twitter account is @legaltweets, where she captures the attention of lawyers and others who are interested in the law and is able to promote her legal writing, including her blogs. She has 11,000-plus followers here and is listed as one of the Top Legal Professionals on Twitter.

Niki's third Twitter account is her personal one, called @nikiblack. Here she shares information about the intersection of law and technology, including cloud and mobile computing and social media, and occasionally shares personal activities, including dinner menus with photos. This account has more than 16,000 followers.

As you can see, Niki loves to write, and whether it is a book, a column, a blog, or a tweet, she is sharing it all on social media. Everything she does crosses from one platform to another.

"In terms of my professional career, I felt that everything initially came from that original blog because I created a body of work. I use Twitter to share my blog as well as other topical information. And because of that, many lawyers know who I am. Social media helped me get back into the legal field and has taken me down this path to where I am now."

From 2005 until the present, Niki's career has grown because of social media. "I never would have accomplished this without social media. Without it, I would have been sitting here in Rochester with a virtual shingle doing contracts, appellate briefs, research, and writing for local lawyers."

Niki uses Facebook, Google+, and LinkedIn and shares presentations she has made with the hundreds of people in her networks as well as links to her books and various accounts such as Twitter, her website, her blog, and other platforms. "There's a Google+ Group that I created and a community for lawyers in the Cloud. Social media is part of what I do now on a daily basis."

Often when lawyers begin using social media, they approach it without a strategy. But for those lawyers just beginning to think about social media, it might be a good idea for them to develop a strategy to quickly incorporate it into their marketing plans. Niki did not start with a strategy, either. "With my blog, I tried to figure out different posts that would interest and engage people, that would compel them to share them. I share my *Daily Record* articles with my contacts on Twitter. It wasn't a conscious strategy, but I created a brand by doing all those things [while] trying to create a niche for myself."

Niki's greatest frustration in using social media is the volume and number of platforms available today. "I'm sure novice social media users are finding this daunting, too. It seems the greatest benefit of networking and building relationships is also the hardest thing to control." Social media provides users with great platforms to build their reputation and their network, but as it grows, it is harder to continue on a one-on-one basis. "Sometimes I feel that I don't pay enough attention to people or interact enough with people [that follow me]. I'm not on all the platforms that I should be. With social media, there is always a new platform coming along. I'm trying to maintain my level of interactivity and still be genuine and not too mechanical about it."

There is a lot to like about social media, particularly when it has been a way to transform your career. Niki says it has given her opportunities she would not have had otherwise. "I like all the people that I've met and connected with. There are so many people all across the country—the world, really—that I consider friends. Some I have met in person that I would never have met in a million years otherwise. It's great for developing relationships, friendships, colleagues, and partnerships."

That is a really great message. Because of social media, Niki developed followers and contacts, built relationships, and was able to share information that was of value to other people. It isn't about her. That is one of the key aspects of social media. It is about others.

What is Niki's advice to other women lawyers? "It's a wonderful medium and they need to use it. It's an opportunity for women lawyers to create something for themselves, to empower themselves, to be someone in the firm that not only does the work but who brings in business, particularly if they use it strategically."

Conclusion

Historically, it took lawyers years to develop a solid legal reputation, but lawyers who are smart *and* willing to embrace social media are doing so much earlier in their careers.

Although it's tempting to want to jump into social media and test the waters, it would behoove lawyers to put together a strategy first. A strategy requires that you understand what each platform's purpose is and what it can do for you. Then plan how you can best use it to get your message out, build your reputation as an expert, and attract business.

Tracking where new business is coming from, how they heard of you, and whether they saw any of your social media before contacting you is important for measuring your impact, time spent, and social media's value to you.

Social media is the key to expanding networks and sharing information in today's world. It is not selling per se, but by using the various platforms, a lawyer can create a profile that distinguishes her from others based on experience and encourages viewers to connect to her. Through regular communication, by sharing valuable information and educating prospects, lawyers are beginning to reap the rewards of new business from social media.

Chapter 4

Communications

Jeanne R. Lee

We have long considered communication to be the exchange of thoughts, opinions, and ideas.[1] Often, we think of communication as the simple conversations and correspondence between two parties. Mastering these techniques is critical to our success—and so is broadening our understanding of effective communication to productively leverage all of our assets as rainmakers.

First, it is critical to understand the many ways that communication pervades—and sometimes prevents—our success. As children, we begin our immersion into communication by learning basic words and their pronunciations, and eventually their synonyms. We expand on this understanding by learning delivery skills: posture, presentation, persuasion, and more. However, these tactics are inherently self-focused, and effective communication involves a dialogue between at least two people. This means also understanding how the other parties are conveying their own information as well as perceiving ours. We learn how to read body language and, hopefully, how to listen, as well.

But effective rainmaking often involves another critical component, which is employing third-party communication channels. These can include branding, marketing, and the use of social media to build a reputation within the community.

In this communications chapter, I will examine how seven successful rainmakers built their practices in such far-ranging locations as Shanghai, Los Angeles, the Midwest, and the East Coast. Their firms are of different sizes and span completely different areas of law.

---

1. The word *communication* is the 37th most popular word on Merriam-Webster.com (October 2014).

Each rainmaker has developed her unique style during her career, and each one used a particular blend of the communication components discussed above. There is no "one size fits all" to building a successful practice, but there are common themes among all seven women.

First, you must be comfortable with who you are, what you stand for, and what your core values are, and you must be genuinely interested in serving the client. Genuineness is being who you are without a façade: "what you see is what you get." You have committed to be honest and open in all conversations.

> *"You must be comfortable with who you are, what you stand for, and what your core values are, and you must be genuinely interested in serving the client."*

In addition, you must be aware of your own communication style and how you can adapt your style to maximize the potential connection with a client. Some attorneys are introverts and operate much better in conducting the majority of their meetings in one-to-one settings. More extroverted attorneys can conduct business well in busy atmospheres. The key is to know which setting best allows you and your client to communicate effectively.

Once you understand the setting that best suits you with client contact, you must then figure out the communication style of your client. One helpful tool is the Personal Styles Coaching Inventory (PSCI), developed by CoachWorks International, in Dallas, Texas. It sets forth four personal styles: director, mediator, presenter, and strategist. In a quick summary:

1. Directors are results oriented and tend to have a tone and pace that is quicker than average. Because of their results orientation, they are natural leaders, but people who come into contact with them may experience them as having rather an abrupt style and find working with them to be stressful.

2. Mediators are the people that everyone likes because they are so personable. Mediators shy away from being the center of attention and their focus is to make everyone feel comfortable.

3. Unlike the mediators, the presenters love being the center of attention. They are great conversationalists, energetic, and generally entertaining, but their follow-though may need prompting on projects.

4. The strategists are hard-working and extremely thorough in their work. They are detail oriented and great problem solvers. Their colleagues experience them as "perfectionists."

Understanding your style and that of your client is critical to quickly building rapport. For example, a director has a fast-paced speaking, thinking, and action style. If a director attorney is meeting with a strategist client whose natural pace is slower and more methodical,

"You must be aware of your own communication style and how you can adapt your style to maximize the potential connection with a client."

the client may not feel a connection to the attorney, and therefore may not retain that attorney if each is engaged in her natural style. However, if the director attorney has a self-awareness of the strengths and liabilities of her style and of the client's, the attorney can adapt her style during the meeting: slowing her pace, allowing the client time to absorb information, and therefore optimizing the potential for a connection and better understanding the client.

Once the rainmaker is with the client in a setting in which she is comfortable, the conversation, focused on what the client would like to speak about, begins. The advice for you to remember is that it is your responsibility to take the steps allowing the conversation to move forward. The simplest way is to be a good listener. Ask yourself the following:

1. Are you multitasking or fully present with the client and conversation? Have you turned off all electronic devices? Have you eliminated all distractions and picked an ideal setting for the conversation?
2. Can you follow the client's form of communication even though the thoughts are not completely in order and perhaps may even seem random?
3. Are you able to reserve judgment as the story unfolds?
4. Are you keeping an open mind about the person?
5. Are you asking questions that invite the potential client to participate in a conversation with you?
6. Does your vocal tone, pace, and volume match that of the client?
7. Are your comments accepting, respectful, and supportive of the client's perspectives?

8. What type of active listening questions do you have in your toolbox to show the client that you are tracking the conversation? (For example, Can you clarify this for me? Is it okay if I put that in different terms to make sure we are talking about the same thing? What I heard you say is this . . . Is that correct? I am not sure if I understood you; could you say it in a different way? Can you put it in another way? What I am hearing you say is . . . Is that accurate?)

9. Are your questions or responses validating of the client's experience?

10. What is your body language saying? What is the client's body language saying?

Once you have identified your and your client's communication style, found a setting that is conducive to a connecting conversation, and engaged in active listening, the final step to creating great communications centers on your ability to be empathic to the client's agenda. From your client's viewpoint, have you been able to listen to what the client says and understand accurately and with sensitivity? Are you able to validate the feelings of the client so that she feels understood? If so, you have met an important component for building a connection—hopefully a long-term connection—to the client.

Next you must develop methods to stay connected to the client. This can be around scheduled quarterly updates or whatever periodicity is appropriate. You can send articles that would be of interest to that individual—schedule coffee, lunches, or phone calls—or send your monthly newsletter.

Whatever strategy you choose to maintain a connection with the client, you must be consistent in the implementation. The majority of rainmakers featured here note that your success in rainmaking will be limited if you do not do what you say you are going to do, or if you fail to follow through in keeping up with the relationships. As several of the attorneys interviewed suggested, it is the failure to follow through that hinders many potentially successful rainmakers.

Keep in mind that developing and maintaining these relationships also relies on your reputation as an attorney: the one you build for yourself and the one that you maintain. This can include social media and continuing to manage your relationships with clients through such platforms as LinkedIn and Facebook, as well as building your brand by keeping track of Yelp, AVVO, and other review sites.

Let's turn to the interviews with the rainmakers.

Esther H. Lim
Partner, Finnegan, Henderson,
Farabow, Garrett & Dunner LLP

Intellectual Property

Esther Lim has specialized in intellectual property internationally for years. Her writings and lectures on the procurement and enforcement of U.S. intellectual property rights cover such specialties as litigation, prosecution, counseling, licensing, due diligence, and portfolio management. This expertise, in addition to being a founding managing partner at Finnegan, Henderson, Farabow, Garrett & Dunner LLP's Shanghai office, is a tribute to Esther's successful communication strategies. "When I was first asked by the chair of the firm if I would open the office in Shanghai, it came as a complete surprise. I asked, 'Do you know that I'm not Chinese?'" She even suggested that the chair look for someone else. It took another year for Esther and her husband, John Yang, who is also an attorney, to accept the offer and another year to move to China. She has been there since 2008.

Esther was in her second trimester of pregnancy when they arrived in Shanghai. For two months, she studied Chinese while opening the office but flew back to Washington, DC, to give birth. Two months later, she flew back to China with her infant daughter. She continues to live in Shanghai with her husband and now two young daughters.

When I asked Esther how she navigates being an American lawyer in China, she said, "It takes time to build relationships, so ongoing communication is necessary. You really need to listen without interjecting your own standards and biases. Understand your audience when you speak. For example, are you adapting your style to the audience? Do you need to speak slower? Have they had experience with patents, and are you speaking at a level they can understand? Have you given clear examples? Are you using PowerPoint visuals? Are you asking questions to get feedback on their understanding of the material? I also keep in touch with clients. I don't have a set tickler system, but I might call or

> *"You really need to listen without interjecting your own standards and biases."*

email to see how they are doing and include relevant updates. I pay attention to my clients and their issues."

It is evident that Esther's ability to succeed in this environment is partly dependent on how she presents herself: "I am an active listener, an introvert, and a deliberate speaker. I tend to speak to add to the conversation. I have found ways that work for me. I am energized in smaller settings. For example, women generally enjoy conversing and eating, so I sometimes take them to high tea.

"In the United States, I spent about 10 percent of my time on marketing, but in China I spend much more time with outreach to companies, associations, government, and schools. In the Shanghai office, there are three resident attorneys and five support staff. We also have attorneys from the U.S. offices who come on a rotating basis for about a month. Those that come here usually speak Mandarin."

Esther has an editorial outlet as the editor-in-chief of *Last Month at the Federal Circuit*, Finnegan's monthly newsletter distributed to subscribers worldwide. "It's a nice way for me to stay abreast of current IP developments, remain connected to contacts, and work with associates on the newsletter," says Esther.

While Esther does not formally track if the newsletter brings in clients, her work with the publication has garnered her some international traction: "I was in Korea recently for a deposition, and a high-level IP director of a client recognized me as the editor of the Finnegan newsletter."

When I asked Esther for recommendations, she gave a variety for her fellow rainmakers. She highly recommends activity in bar associations (she became actively involved as a second-year associate), noting that these give the opportunity to both work with and give back to the community—in addition to yielding meaningful connections. She also points out how important it is to understand her various audiences, and that she had to work to understand the differences between American and Chinese organizations. She says, "In China, I often present at seminars, visit associations and government agencies, and teach at universities. These activities are not done for the express purpose of rainmaking, but one of the natural consequences is rainmaking. People appreciate useful information and learning, and they appreciate your efforts." She pauses for a moment, adding that you have to be patient. "Sometimes it takes years to develop a relationship."

Women especially can take advantage of their communication skills, says Esther. "Women are good communicators, and particularly strong with nonverbal cues. Use nonverbal feedback to understand the client. A woman shouldn't apologize for not competing with a more aggressive style. As women, we bring views and life experiences that provide additional perspectives. Just make sure you have something relevant to say."

Esther's final words are an encouragement to professional women everywhere, in every field: "It is common for women to share credit (and use the word *we* for success) and to own blame (and use the word *I* for taking responsibility for mistakes). Be more cognizant as credits and responsibilities are discussed. Be proactive. Get credit for what you deserve and don't take a back seat."

Esther and I are at the end of our virtual "high tea," me in Denver, Esther in Shanghai. Esther communicates a wry wit over the phone: "Almost 30 years after I emigrated from Korea to the United States, I am now one hour away from where I was born. So I haven't gone very far, but what a world of difference."

Harmeet Kaur Dhillon
Partner, Dhillon & Smith LLP
General and Complex Commercial Litigation; Campaign and Election Law; Intellectual Property (Trademark, Copyright, and Trade Secrets); Securities Litigation; Corporate Governance Issues; Civil Rights and Civil Liberties; First Amendment (Right of Publicity, Slander, Defamation, Trade Libel, and anti-SLAPP); Entertainment Transactions and Litigation

In November 2013, Harmeet Dhillon celebrated the seventh anniversary of her firm Dhillon & Smith—a firm that now has ten attorneys. Harmeet had been practicing for about ten years—including jobs with large firms and as clerk in the United States Fourth Circuit Court of Appeals (the Honorable Paul V. Niemeyer)—when she decided to open her own office.

Harmeet immediately recognized that the first critical component to communicating was communicating who and what she was to a larger audience. Her marketing strategy initially included word of mouth that she had gone out on her own, mostly networking with friends and former colleagues at lunches and cocktail events. But ultimately, Harmeet adds, it was getting a couple of *good clients* who referred others that got her practice "off and running."

Harmeet specializes in general and complex commercial litigation, First Amendment litigation (including anti-SLAPP), election and campaign law and compliance, employment law and discrimination litigation, securities and regulatory compliance, Internet law, and intellectual property. In the beginning, however, she focused on doing a lot of pro bono work in the employment area. "I mean *a lot,*" she states, and eventually people began to pay her for the employment work she had done previously for free. Today employment work makes up 25 percent of the firm's practice and keeps two associates busy full-time.

Harmeet's current strategies to stay out front include the use of Yelp, LinkedIn, Facebook, and AVVO, although Yelp is a relatively new addition to the firm's communication strategy. Harmeet's use of these third-party communication channels embodies the need to expand our understanding of communication to be successful rainmakers: "I'm active on Facebook and LinkedIn, but we do not have a firm newsletter. I have about 2,000 friends on my personal Facebook page and about 250 on our business page. I post on my Facebook page three to four times a week. I will post a legal article that I think would be interesting, what I am doing (yes, 'I am just getting out of court and . . . '), or what our firm is focusing on that week. What I post always has a legal flavor to it. I will often have people tell me they didn't know I practiced in an area until they saw me post something on Facebook, and then they hire me. With respect to LinkedIn, I post something at least once a week about what I'm doing; however, I am more active on Facebook than LinkedIn."

The firm is also active on AVVO—with about 60-plus reviews— and Harmeet has been able to get these reviews by asking her clients to take five minutes to post a review. This communication tool not only offers Harmeet direct feedback from her clients about their satisfaction but also helps build and maintain a two-way loyalty street. She also has about 26 endorsements from attorneys. "I have never had anyone say no, though not everyone you ask will take the time to post," she says. If there is a negative review, AVVO will notify her, but "there will always be clients who are not happy, and I have to consider the attorney-client privilege."

Harmeet notes that the types of clients her firm gets through AVVO are related to employment matters. "If the matter has been referred to us from someone we know, I have my associates do a first review," she says. "With respect to all other employment matters, I generally do a first review because 50 percent of employment leads would not be good cases for us to take on." On AVVO she has a personal rating of 10/10 for being a top employment lawyer and a top litigation lawyer.

Harmeet says she does not do exit interviews. "I am in close contact with my clients, and I know immediately if there is any dissatisfaction. When there is, I address it immediately. I give outstanding client service because the vast majority of referrals have come from former clients and are rounded out by friends and colleagues and opposing counsel." In other words, Harmeet emphasizes open communication throughout the process, as opposed to bookending the experience with information garnering.

Recently, Harmeet made history by becoming the first woman elected to the position of vice chair of the California Republican Party. She has an impressive history that helped her get here. She arrived from India when she was two years old. She attended Dartmouth College, where she earned a bachelor of arts degree in classical studies (ancient Greek, Latin, classical art, and archaeology), and the University of Virginia, where she received her law degree and sat on the editorial board of the *Virginia Law Review*.

She is now the second most powerful Republican in the state of California party leadership. "I get a lot of free publicity from being the vice chair," she says. "The media will ask me to comment on various issues we are facing, like now I am asked to comment on immigration and Obamacare. Because I have won various awards that demonstrate my commitment to public interest issues—my work with civil rights and human rights—I am reinforced in certain markets as a good lawyer and a good person."

When asked what advice she would give to others on how to make it rain, Harmeet has a ready answer: "I consistently spend about an hour a day on marketing. Take a long-term view. Not everything pays off immediately. Meet your deadlines. Be a good lawyer. Don't waste people's time—people respect that. Speak as an expert where potential clients will be present. Build relationships with attorneys who can refer business to you. I don't do social gatherings after work. I make myself available for lunches, and people know this. Socializing after work is a challenge for women because that is what men do: they go out after work. But I have made a decision not to socialize after work. I have work with the Republican Party and I spend time with my husband. People know this and respect it. And they know that I will make myself available for lunch."

Grace Parke Fremlin

Partner, Steptoe & Johnson LLP

International Trade and Investment;
Corporate, Securities and Finance;
International Regulation and Compliance;
Renewable and Alternative Energy;
Intellectual Property Litigation/Transactions;
Entertainment

Grace Parke Fremlin is a partner and cochair of the Korea Practice at Steptoe & Johnson LLP in the Washington, DC, office. She specializes in government relations and policy as well as international transactions (inbound and outbound commercial investments with Korea, China, Hong Kong, and Japan), specifically involving global supply and the procurement of goods and services, foreign direct investments, and company mergers and acquisitions. When Grace joined the firm in late 2005, Steptoe had no Korea practice. Today, the Korea practice has revenue in the tens of millions of dollars, is flourishing, and covers attorneys in multiple practice areas.

In 2005, the U.S. and Korean governments announced they would negotiate a U.S.-Korea free trade agreement (FTA). Grace states, "We sought the representation of the Korean government in the U.S.-Korea FTA and we won the plum engagement. This seminal representation of the Korean government by Steptoe (followed by work on the Korea-EU FTA and multiple others consummated by Korea) launched our Korea practice. Internally, I approached the most senior and highly ranked international trade partner, and he was gung-ho about starting a Korea practice. Timing was perfect and strategic: I already had a relationship with the Korean government, the firm possessed the highest reputation and ranking possible in international trade, and there was a distinct and immediate need for legal services in this area."

She notes that all three elements must be present and converge for a successful rainmaking: relationship with the target, reputation of the firm in the needed legal specialty, and relevance of the legal specialty to the client. "First, you must build a relationship or have a relationship with the company or organization," says Grace. "You must be in touch with the decision maker or someone who can get you to that person. Cold calling does not work, especially in Asia. When the client brings a need or demand to you, you must match the reputation of the firm and then look to see what relevant work you can do for the client."

Next, Grace advises, "You must keep the relationship fresh and current. You must visit, have meetings, phone calls, emails, lunches, and dinners. These should be as frequent as possible. In some ways, having to target relationships across the Pacific Ocean forced me to map out, preplan, and maximize every minute of my infrequent trips to Seoul, especially in the early years of the launch of our Korea practice. You have to be driven, patient, and caring, all at the same time. It's a lot of work."

Grace suggests that if you see that a suit has been filed against a company with whom you have a relationship, pick up the phone and call, or email first so that they are alerted to the litigation and then call the client "because you already have a relationship." Have the following conversation: "I saw that a suit has been filed against you. We have experience in precisely this type of litigation and wondered if we could present our capabilities to assist you."

Generally, she says, in a litigation matter where the Asian companies are most often defendants, the reply is "Yes, we are looking" or "We are starting a request for proposal [RFP]" or "Yes, please send us a proposal."

"In a corporate investment or merger/acquisition scenario, the situation is confidential, and it is less of an open game," says Grace. "You have to rely more on the firm's high ranking and reputation in M&A [mergers and acquisitions], coupled with the relationship. Otherwise, even if you get wind of a transaction soon enough, you will not get on the shortlist."

Once you have the relationship, Grace notes, you must deepen and broaden it. "As your base broadens, your reputation naturally spreads within the organization. Once you get that first engagement and you deliver a great outcome or quality performance, it gets immensely easier. It is no longer about originating a new client; it is about proliferating additional matters for an existing client. You are no longer climbing up the hill; you are now rolling downhill like a snowball."

Grace points out that follow-up is best if it is strategic.

"In strategic follow-up," she says, "you are asking the following questions: (1) Why are you targeting them? (2) What do they need that is a match with your or the firm's strengths? and (3) Is the client's need and your strength or the firm's strength in high demand and in a hot growth area that makes proliferation of additional matters possible? Be thoughtful about your follow-up, remembering that where people are today (in a company or outside the company) may not be where they are tomorrow."

Grace points out that there are communication strategies that women may be particularly good at: "Have confidence to go after the business for others, not just for yourself. 'Cross-marketing' is an area in which women can excel and may be more willing to initiate than men. Men are more likely to sell only their own expertise. Their first question may be 'What's in it for me?' This is not the right question to ask when you are trying to build a new practice group, particularly a multidisciplinary one," she says. "Using a softer sell in internal contexts is a plus because you are already known. We fail to get business not because we lack relationships but because of the failure to follow up. Keep focused on the long term, be always on the lookout for those opportunities when your three Rs line up, and be ready to hit a home run. Finally, stay in the game. You cannot hit a home run if you are out of the game."

Women can be excellent at marketing and helping each other, notes Grace; they are natural collaborators. "I didn't build this practice group on my own. I partnered with another cochair, the international trade partner that worked with me to land the Korean government representation, and together we went after the legal work from major Korean business conglomerates, referred to as *chaebols* by Koreans. Because of the natural collaboration of women, women support each other. Some of my lucky breaks in building a Korea practice at Steptoe have been from Korean in-house women lawyers. They may not always be the decision makers, but they can connect me to them or help me with leads or advice." This trend of increasing women lawyers in-house is occurring everywhere and could in time be a game changer.

Grace encourages women to focus on relationships where the affinity is natural. "Men talk about sports and banter back and forth. It is hard for most women to participate in that conversation. If you are one of the few women who loves sports, great; but if you are not, take a different path. Golf, sports, and drinking are not the only paths to rainmaking."

Whether you are male or female, rainmaking is hard work, Grace observes. "Make the effort, be thoughtful and strategic. Be thoughtful of what legal specialty is your brand and how it matches up with your firm's strengths. Finally, your legal specialty and your firm's strengths should match up with the legal needs of your relationships now and into the future. In short, pick a hot area of the law or a future hot area of the law. In my case, I picked thriving countries—Japan and Korea in the '80s, Hong Kong and China in the '90s, China and Korea in the early 2000s, and exclusively Korea since arriving at Steptoe in 2005. It has to be a conscious and strategic endeavor."

In sum, she says, "Remember that rainmaking can come from your family and friends. Or, it can be earned based on the merits of the three Rs. Either way, or both, it's a game worth pursuing. And, soon, an era when women are disadvantaged at this game will be gone."

Judy Man-Ling Lam

Litigation Partner, Kumagai Law Group PC

Complex Business Disputes, Particularly in the Areas of Real Estate, Banking, Business Torts, Fraud Schemes, and Franchise Litigation

I am catching Judy Lam, a partner at Greenberg Glusker Fields Claman & Machtinger LLP in Los Angeles, on a cell phone as she is between the end of one client meeting and a luncheon. She has been practicing for 20 years, primarily as a litigator. Prior to law school, she worked for four years in the banking industry. I am particularly excited to learn about her multifaceted approach to successful client communication because she is well known for tailoring her skills to her client's best advantage, and for their best interests, in their particular cases, whether it is aggressive litigation or skillful negotiation.

"My practice is very dependent on referrals from bankers and CPAs," says Judy. "I have a trusted adviser role in these relationships. I stay in contact with these groups and let them know the type of cases I'm working on, and I let my contacts know the type of cases I would like them to send to me and in what situations they should call me."

From the very beginning, Judy worked at firms where she had mentors who encouraged her to develop business. Going out to events was not hard for her. "I naturally like social events," she says.

For beginning rainmakers, she recommends starting out in inti-mate settings like one-on-ones, particularly for introverts. "Bring a buddy," says Judy. "Just take the initiative and make a plan for your-self. I like meeting interesting people. So I do, and I try to get to the National Association of Women Business Owners. I have found that younger women are a warm audience. I also stay involved in groups where bankers, real estate agents, and franchise people are. I take leadership roles in organizations, and I am active in bar sections and attend bar conventions."

Judy says she spends about 30 percent of her time marketing, which is more time than other attorneys. She serves on panels, pub-lishes articles, and is involved in the community. "I don't keep track of where my business is coming from, but I do have a lot of referrals from the same sources and repeat work from corporations. I do not have a formal exit interview."

Forty percent of her practice focuses on Asian companies, and she has a keen interest in helping clients resolve conflicts—not just basing the relationship on applying the law.

When I ask Judy what communication advice she would give to her fellow rainmakers, she says, "Pick a mode of communication that is natural to you. The mode has to be authentic to you. Use that mode consistently to keep in contact with clients, whether it is by email, phone, or meeting in person. Just be consistent."

Margaret W. Wong

President and Managing Partner,
Margaret W. Wong & Associates, LPA
Immigration Law

In 1950, Margaret W. Wong was born in the former British colony of Hong Kong. Months earlier, her Chinese parents had fled the politi-cal repression of civil war caused by the Com-munist takeover of China. Margaret came to the United States on a study visa at age 19 and brought her 18-year-old sister with her. She attended a small college in Iowa. She had few belongings and no money.

Upon graduation, she went to Buffalo Law School in New York and graduated in 1976. She became one of the first foreign-born female lawyers to be admitted to practice law in New York and Ohio. She applied for positions for nine months before she got her first job. She then had several jobs and ultimately was fired from her last job because "I could not understand the United States culture."

"I had no choice but to start my own law firm," says Margaret. "I was fired. I had no plan. I started with a $25 desk, no secretary, and no clients." She began walking the streets and handing out her business cards to people on the sidewalk and on buses. Today her law firm, Margaret W. Wong & Associates, is housed in a state-of-the-art building that the firm owns in Cleveland, Ohio, its headquarters. Margaret W. Wong & Associates has offices in New York, Atlanta, Chicago, Columbus, Detroit, Nashville, and Los Angeles, in addition to its Cleveland office. The firm consists of eight attorneys and a staff of 45 to 50.

Over the past two decades, Margaret has assisted corporations to obtain work visas for their executives and helped individuals to become permanent residents, obtain appropriate papers to work, advance their education, and pursue opportunities in the United States. They also do deportation and asylum, as well as family-based visas. The firm handles every type of immigration problem. The staff is multilingual, with proficiency in English, Mandarin, Cantonese, Hindi, Korean, Russian, Spanish, French, and German. The firm was in the news in December 2013 for its successful bid to allow President Obama's uncle to remain in the United States rather than be deported. The firm previously represented President Obama's sister in her successful bid for a green card in 2010. In January 2014, the firm was also named in *U.S. News & World Report* as one of the best law firms in the United States.

Margaret also has a great deal of personal success. She is the current cochair of the Immigration Law Committee for the National Asian Pacific Bar Association and chair of the Cleveland Bar Association's immigration law section. She is a recipient of numerous awards, including the prestigious Ellis Island Medal of Honor from the Ellis Island Medal of Honor Society, Ohio Chapter, which she received in 1998, and in February 2013 she was awarded the Edward F. Jaeckle Award, the highest award bestowed by the Buffalo Law School of New York and Law School Alumni Association. She is also an adjunct professor of law at Case Western Reserve University, an honorary professor at the People's University of China, an inductee into the Ohio Women's Hall of Fame, a recipient of the Rotary Club International's Service Award, a life member of the Eighth Judicial District Court and the Federal Sixth Circuit Court, and a recipient of the Trailblazer Award from the National Asian Pacific American Bar Association. She is also the author of *The Immigrant's Way*.

"First, make your clients glad that they chose you," says Margaret, when I ask what communication strategies have helped her become such a successful rainmaker. "Educate them thoroughly and always show them you care. I engage only in straight talk and expect that from my staff."

She continues, "You have to do what you say you are going to do. Say it and then do it! I answer all my phone calls and emails the same day, even if this means doing so late at night. If the client is not happy, I deal with it. I will take whatever necessary steps to make sure the client is represented well. I have, on my own dollar, flown to see my clients wherever they are located, including visiting jails. Ninety percent of having a profitable practice is making the clients happy. Most of my practice comes from referrals from past clients (60 percent). If a case is denied, really communicate with the client. Again, educate them continuously about their case and let them know you care. Immigration law is complicated, and our clients are sophisticated and intelligent. They are always Googling and researching on their own.

"The craft of the lawyer is to have the time to be creative," says Margaret. "It is not marketing. People hire you because of you. Listen well and work very hard. Build your partnerships, support your associates, and help other people. Take every small job and work it hard. Make those calls. Write that memo."

Margaret is extremely active in her community as a leader, mentor, and philanthropist. Her colleagues attest that she is not a person whose name simply appears as a committee member—she is an active participant.

> *"Educate them [the client] continuously about their case and let them know you care."*

I asked Margaret how she is able to accomplish what she does—growing her firm, being a manager and a mother, and being extremely active in her community.

"When I was younger, I did a lot of managing," says Margaret. "Now I trust others more. I am in the office by 5 or 5:15 a.m. and I stay very late. When my children were younger (now they are lawyers), my husband and family were a big help. Now I work early and I work late. I return calls and emails late at night."

"There is no work-life balance," Margaret explains. "It is a struggle. Successful people do not think about work-life balance. Just do it. There is more guilt if you think about it." She pauses for a moment. "Sometimes it is difficult to get up in the morning. But you do it."

I ask Margaret about her extended communication strategy, including how she markets. "I spend about 3 to 5 percent of my time on marketing," says Margaret. "I also have an assistant who helps me now. I have three radio talk shows, two in Chinese and one in Spanish. Each occurs every week. I also send out 10,000-plus holiday cards each year and throw a Christmas party that about 500 to 600 people attend."

Finally, when I asked Margaret what else she could share about how she is successful, she did not even pause: "God is with me. Luck. Great people. My mom. She was a tiger mom. She taught us discipline. She had a passion for other people. She taught me, if you can help, then why not?"

With her passion to assist other immigrants and her own firsthand experience through the immigration process, Margaret certainly has become a beacon of light and hope to those who want to make America their home.

Dana Perry

Shareholder, Chambliss, Bahner & Stophel, PC

Estate Planning, Special Needs Planning, Elder Law

Dana Perry, a shareholder in the law firm of Chambliss, Bahner & Stophel, PC, realized early in her practice that her clients needed a clear explanation of what their legal documents said. They needed help navigating the legal system. She drafted customized explanations that clearly set out "here's what it says; here's what it means; here's what still needs to be done—a road map."

She did this in response to a perceived need—a gap in the services they'd been getting.

"When you work with families as your clients, it's the opposite of a 'one-up' engagement," says Dana. "You need to build a long-term relationship. Estate planning needs to be revisited on a regular basis."

This is just one example of Dana's hands-on approach to helping clients provide for their families' future security and protection of assets through creative planning.

When Dana inherited a client, she would look through the existing paperwork in their files for a plan but often didn't find anything. She realized they needed a document that would "describe their world—make sense of every legal instrument, such as wills, trusts, pre-existing trusts, a private foundation. A master document condenses everything into plain English that serves as a key resource for both family and any lawyers who worked with them."

Her template for this evolved over time. She found that her clients loved the document for how it "cut through the clutter."

This documentation became an integral part of the client's plan and was a big selling point for Dana's services. It differentiated her in that she could point out that she would not just be generating legal documents but would also ensure that the client really understood what the plan was and what those documents meant. "Wealthy clients are judicious in choosing who they want handling their affairs," says Dana.

For each client, she strives to determine the best way to make the information clear. It might be in Word format, it might be Excel spreadsheets, or it might be a PowerPoint presentation.

Dana's current firm has about 60 lawyers and a variety of practice groups. She helped get across to other partners that estate planning isn't just a standalone area—it can also apply to clients in many other areas. Before, that area wasn't considered as very important. She helped her partners see beyond the accepted way of doing things. Dana herself specializes in long-term care planning, navigating Medicaid rules, veterans' benefits planning, multigenerational trust planning, and drafting and administering supplemental needs trusts.

Dana espoused building a client base and cross-selling her firm's services. Estate planning should lead to work in other areas, she believes. In that way, estate planning lawyers become "givers" of work to other areas.

Dana also looks strategically at technology tools. "How do you translate tech issues so that you can communicate in a way that's permanent and that clients understand what it is they're signing?" An ongoing issue she has faced with new clients is that when she discusses documents they signed five years ago, they claim they didn't understand what they were signing.

The road maps she constructs are planning memos. They may include flow charts for those clients who are visual learners. "The key is to look at what you're doing as outward looking in, not as inward looking out," says Dana. "Think about it from the client's perspective; put yourself in their shoes. You have the information they need, so give them what they want in a manner that is most useful to them and fits their individual needs."

Dana speaks about once a month, which forces her to continue learning. "If you can talk about it, you can better communicate it to the judge or to your clients." She writes client alerts for the firm website to show she's keeping up with the latest developments in her field. She uses Twitter to further circulate alerts. She spends about an hour a day on writing, outreach to clients, preparation for speaking engagements, and so on. She thinks some women feel they juggle so much that they have to cut out something, so they focus only on legal work and don't do the outreach they should.

"That's a mistake," says Dana. "There are two kinds of lawyers— lawyers who have clients, and lawyers who depend on other lawyers for work. You want to have your own clients. By year two or three of practice, you should start thinking about how to bring in your own business. And you can never stop—you have to keep at it for the remainder of your career. You must be strategic about it."

Diana King and Paula Greisen

Partners, King & Greisen LLP

Employment and Civil Rights Law

The law firm of King & Greisen is located near the inner-city school of East High in Denver, Colorado, and is housed in a Victorian house. But there is nothing Victorian about the two partners of this highly regarded female-owned law firm that opened in 2002. Paula Greisen grew up in a small town in Virginia, where her mother served as a court watcher for the local legal aid society making sure that defendants' rights were not violated. Her mom and her family were open about their beliefs and convictions, and Paula only understood years later how unique it was to be open with those convictions, especially for her mom, as a woman in that time period. So, from an early age, Paula knew that she would represent the underdog in some way. Paula

attended the University of Oklahoma and received a degree in geo-
logical engineering and then went on to University of Colorado law
school. During law school, Paula interned at a large firm and realized
that it was not fulfilling to work on cases that she "did not have an
emotional connection with."

Diane grew up with a father who was a psychologist and assumed
that she also would be one. She is a self-proclaimed "Air Force brat"—
born in Texas and lived in California, Oklahoma, and Guam. She
attended middle school and high school in Fort Collins and then went
to Colorado State University. While working as a volunteer coun-
selor, she decided that "if I could take one thing that wasn't working for a client and fix it, that
would be rewarding." She later
decided on law and got her JD
at the University of California, Berkeley. She came back
to Denver and chose a large
law firm that emphasized pro
bono work. It was through her pro bono work that her passion for
civil rights and justice became cemented, and ultimately she opened
up her own law firm.

> *"Win your cases so that you communicate your passion and mission."*

Diane and Paula have both served as president to the faculty of
Federal Advocates; on the boards of directors of numerous organizations, including Colorado legal services; as treasurer for the National
Employment Lawyer's Association, the Colorado Plaintiffs Employment Lawyers Association, and the American Civil Liberties Union;
and on the Merit Selection Panel and Committee on Conduct for the
United States District Court.

So, it is no surprise that the two women ultimately brought their
collective experience, commitment for the civil liberties of all individuals, and passion for justice to the law firm they have today—King
& Greisen. King & Greisen fights for the protection of individuals' civil
rights and liberties. They firmly believe that no person should be treated
differently because of his or her age, gender, race, religion, national ori-
gin, disability, veteran status, or sexual orientation. In keeping with
their commitment to these issues, the lawyers at King & Greisen regularly volunteer their time to legal and community organizations.

The firm chooses its cases carefully. *Really carefully.* In fact, they
turn away about 80 percent of the ones that come through their front
door. And, even if the potential client gets an initial meeting with an

attorney, the firm may still decline representation unless Diane and Paula have a high degree of confidence in the merits of the case. This is an example of effective, large-scale communication: when King & Greisen takes on a case, the clear message to the community is that it's a case with legs. Diane and Paula have worked hard to cultivate and maintain this brand, which ultimately helps them as rainmakers and benefits their clients.

Both women agree that their best communication tool is to produce results by winning the cases they take on, which creates a powerful reputation in the community. It is important to them that when opposing counsel knows they are on a case, they start from the premise that there is a strong likelihood that the claims have merit. Paula explains, "We carefully select our cases. We work them hard. By the time opposing counsel gets a letter from us, we have all our ducks in a row. Because we have the reputation of being extremely selective in what we will take, opposing counsel 'knows that it is serious.'"

Paula goes on to say: "We take on cases that we care about, that have the potential to make new law, or where someone has been treated 'fundamentally unfairly.' Our clients range from maintenance workers to CEOs. We don't take cases because they will be easy, but because there are important rights to vindicate."

They have no fear of big opposing parties. Diane won a record verdict on behalf of two longtime employees who argued they were fired because of age and gender discrimination. The employer was Denver Country Club, a very exclusive old moneyed country club in Denver.

Like David, they took on the Goliath of the Colorado Department of Corrections. In that case, an employee claimed she was sexually harassed by her supervisors, and she was then written up for being too compassionate toward inmates and eventually terminated for poor performance. Diane prevailed with a record judgment.

In another case involving Lockheed Martin, which ranked 59 in the Fortune 500, an employee alleged that her boss was using the corporation's pen pal program to have sexual trysts with soldiers and billing the costs back to the government. The federal Occupational Safety and Health Administration dismissed the employees' complaint, but Diane filed a whistle-blower complaint under the Sarbanes-Oxley Act. Again, she prevailed. Yes, she prevailed.

Similarly, Paula took on the state of Colorado in her class-action case against the prison system for failing to accommodate inmates with disabilities. Her legal team won the case in 2003 after an almost decade-long fight.

In December 2013, Paula, as a part of the ACLU's legal team, assisted in getting an administrative ruling that a cake shop in Colorado had no right to refuse an order for a wedding cake for a gay couple. And in October 2013, Paula, on behalf of four women who worked for, or are working at, a well-established and popular sushi spot in Denver, filed an EEOC claim based on the female workers claiming harassment and discrimination at the restaurant.

Both women also stand up for individual rights regardless of the size of the perpetrator of the discrimination, and they have done so successfully and against huge odds. Their willingness to take on big challenges while also being very discriminating in the facts of the cases communicates the effectiveness and message of their practice for them.

The women also state that 40 to 50 percent of their referrals come from defense counsel. Diane says, "Former clients are also great referral sources, as are other lawyers who do not practice in this area. We like referrals from defense counsel because they usually have done an initial screening for us."

The women also collectively believe that they are able to communicate their expertise through holding leadership roles in the specialty bars and general bar, taking on pro bono cases, mentoring other attorneys, teaching CLE classes, or teaching in the community. This helps keep them in the public eye.

At the end of the interview, I asked them what they would tell other women to employ in addition to their communication strategy described above so that they can be successful rainmakers.

Paula's recommendations: "Partners in firms are not taught how to run a business. Learn the business of running a law practice. In addition, it is important that your resume reflects the values and the work you want to do. Volunteer or find an internship showing your interests in working for worthy causes."

Diane's recommendations: "Find something that you can be passionate about and pursue it. Writing, interpersonal skills, and being able to evaluate cases are really important skills. Be willing to make sacrifices and work really hard. In the end, it's worth it."

Final recommendations from both Diane and Paula: "Be persistent. If you want something, go for it. Take risks. Knock on doors. Have confidence. Make yourself do it."

Conclusion

As you can see, there is no one absolute way to communicate with your clients. From the law firm of three partners to the traditional large law firm of 500 attorneys, introvert or extrovert, each attorney found her natural style and then adapted her style to the client. Regardless of the natural style used, each rainmaker was genuinely interested in the person first. Without genuine interest in the client, the opportunity for connection decreases, resulting in the potential client not feeling invited to continue a conversation with the lawyer. Finally, the communication is clear, the strategic follow-up occurs to create and/or maintain the relationship, and excellent and timely client services are delivered.

Chapter 5

Writing

Beverly A. Loder

Writing for publication has long been an effective and powerful marketing tool for lawyers. Well before the advent of the Internet and social media, savvy lawyers used writing to raise their profile, build credibility, establish their expertise, and differentiate themselves from their competitors. They wrote articles for legal industry and trade magazines—an excellent way to get their names in front of their peers, referral sources, and most importantly, prospective clients. Many lawyers created newsletters to mail out to their contacts. Still others were fortunate enough to contribute a chapter to a book, or better yet, author an entire book that was printed and distributed by an established legal publisher.

With the explosion of Web-based publications and social media, opportunities to be published now abound. There is no end to the number of websites, online newsletters, blogs, and other publications vying for good content to push out to readers on a daily—even hourly—basis. Most online and many print publications now provide contributor guidelines on their websites that specify the format, length, style, submission instructions, and other particulars for the content they are seeking. Traditional publishers often post book proposal submission guidelines online as well. Some periodicals provide editorial calendars that outline the general topics they plan to cover over the year along with submission deadlines. Once you have thoroughly familiarized yourself with the type of content that is being distributed by a particular publisher or website, you can—and should—use these helpful online resources to better ensure your submission or proposal will be accepted.

The flip side of this is that there is so much content available to readers, it is more important than ever to have a strategic plan in place prior to writing to ensure your content doesn't get overlooked. Who are the targets you most want to reach? What topics are they most interested in—and what are the questions they are asking to be addressed? Which publications are they likeliest to read, and in what format? Would it be better to self-publish a newsletter, blog, or book rather than contribute to an established one? How can you best repurpose a piece once it's published? How will you leverage it? And how will you follow it up with additional published pieces? The answers to these questions should be part of your plan.

Once you have identified the audience, topic, and best vehicles for your writing, it is wise to formally schedule writing time in your calendar rather than attempt to do it on the fly. Depending on the length of the piece, some find it easiest to reserve relatively short blocks of time—say 30 to 60 minutes—two to five days a week until the piece is completed. Others find it more productive to set aside a larger block of time—several hours to a full day—once a week until the task is done. You may have to experiment a while before you settle into a rhythm that works for you and allows you to accomplish your writing goals without throwing off your other priorities. With perseverance, writing can become like any other good habit you've developed and will fit seamlessly into your schedule.

This is not to say it will always come easy. It takes discipline and diligence to develop useful, well-crafted content. Once you do, it's important to leverage your hard work as fully as possible. You should strive to repurpose content using multiple platforms. For example, parts of a longer article can be reworked and used as blog posts. Key points can be pulled out into a bulleted list of items that can be tweeted individually or presented as a checklist on LinkedIn or on your website. An excerpt from the article can be expanded into yet another article with a different focus. The possibilities abound. And, of course, links to the original article should be posted on your website and on all your social media outlets. There should be no excuse for "one and done" when it comes to getting something published. You want to take advantage of every opportunity to get that content out, which will result in exposure to different audiences, particularly when it is shared by others in your social media networks.

> *"Take advantage of every opportunity to get that content out..."*

This is what content marketing entails. But like any kind of marketing, it won't work if the content isn't valuable or, at the very least, interesting. We hear a lot about "thought leadership" these days, and thought leadership is an important component of content marketing. For your content to be effective, it needs to be recognized by your intended audience as insightful and innovative, as well as informative. Don't be intimidated by that. If you consistently use your genuine voice when writing about a topic you know well, and if you authoritatively address the challenges and answer the questions your targeted audience has, you will earn their respect, ideally their business—and eventually the title of "thought leader."

In the pages that follow, we will hear from five women lawyers who have found writing to be a particularly effective way to develop business and grow their respective practices, sometimes in unexpected ways.

Linda J. Ravdin

Partner, Pasternak & Fidis, PC

Family Law

Linda J. Ravdin has used writing as a business development tool for most of her 40 years as a busy family law practitioner. In the mid-1970s, Linda launched a successful solo practice in the District of Columbia, and joined her current firm, the 15-lawyer Pasternak & Fidis, as a partner in 2002. Licensed in Washington, DC, Maryland, and Virginia, Linda focuses her practice on divorce and family law for families of all kinds. She is a nationally known authority on premarital and postmarital agreements.

In the early 1980s, Linda began writing articles for the newsletter of the Women's Bar Association (WBA) of DC. "The editor asked me to write about my experience starting my own practice right out of law school. It ended up as a two-part article," she recalled. "I got a lot of good feedback, other bar members became familiar with me, and I started getting referrals right off the bat. As a result of that experience, I developed a strategy to leverage my writing. I suggested other articles I could write for that newsletter, including a series of five articles about other women who had started their own practices. That's how I started writing regularly. I was also very active in the WBA for a number of years, formed many personal and professional relationships in those early years, many of which I still have, and that's where my business really began to develop."

Over time, other publications sought out Linda's contributions. "Once I realized how easy it was to get published, and how I could use publishing to market my practice, I became very focused on doing as much writing as I could find time to do. It has had a huge impact on my practice. I've never stopped writing, and I've seen consistent results year in and year out."

Linda acknowledges that writing was never the only thing she did to develop business; rather, it's always been a part of a larger game plan. "I also do a lot of CLE presentations," she explained. "The two things go together. They both require that I maintain a high level of knowledge of the subjects I teach and write about. I use material I develop for teaching to write articles and vice versa. Both activities have enabled me to constantly remind potential referral sources of what I do for a living. I also speak to nonlawyer groups whenever I get the chance. Teaching and writing lends credibility. People assume you have exceptional expertise if respected organizations are willing to publish your writings or engage you to teach."

The type of writing Linda does has evolved over the years. Early on, she wrote articles for a variety of legal periodicals and several book chapters for ABA books, including a chapter on collecting fees in the ABA classic *Flying Solo*. "Most of my writing in the early years was about practice management and ethics," Linda explained. "There came a point where I felt I had exhausted those topics and wanted to do more writing about family law, my substantive area of expertise. In the early 1990s I was asked to write a book, *Domestic Relations Manual for the District of Columbia*, which I coauthored with another lawyer, Diane Brenneman, who later became a judge." That book was published by LexisNexis Matthew Bender and continues to be supplemented annually. Since then, Linda has written three additional books, all covering premarital agreements, including the ABA book *Premarital Agreements: Drafting and Negotiation*.

Linda continues to write articles for a number of legal publications, also contributing articles to her firm newsletter on a regular basis. Because drafting premarital agreements and representing clients in divorce who have premarital agreements is an important part of her practice, she focuses most of her writing on that subject because building that niche is the most important aspect of her current marketing strategy.

Linda contends that it's always been easy to find someone who will publish what you've written if it's any good (and sometimes even if it's not). "The hard part is carving out the time to do the work," she says. "Most mornings I go to a coffee shop around 7:30 and I order four shots of espresso. If I have a writing project, or CLE materials to prepare, I spend an hour or so working on it. When I was writing my books, I carved out time on four or five days of every week, both early morning and at other times. For example, for one of the books I was writing, I would read cases on the subway going to the courthouse. At home, I might write for two to three hours on weekends and for an hour or two on some weeknights. The key was working on the writing consistently, week in and week out, even if only for an hour at a time."

> *"Many local bar associations, sections of state bars, and both larger and smaller professional organizations have publications and are always looking for people who will write for them."*

Linda encourages women lawyers to be proactive in seeking out writing opportunities. "Many local bar associations, sections of state bars, and both larger and smaller professional organizations have publications and are always looking for people who will write for them. Call or email the editor of the publication and pitch a story, or ask if they have a theme issue coming up and whether there's an article they are looking for that you could write. Some will not be interested. Some will. Ask about their deadlines, length, style, and other requirements. The best place to start is with a publication of an organization you are already active in. Then, if you are given the opportunity to contribute, be sure to meet your deadline and turn in a polished article. If you do that, it's likely you will be asked to write for them again."

Victoria Pynchon

Author, Speaker, Consultant, Trainer, and Mediator of "She Negotiates," a Consulting and Training Dispute Resolution Company

During her first 24 years in law practice, Victoria Pynchon wrote only one article for publication. Yet she had wanted to write since childhood, pecking away on a Royal typewriter beginning at the tender age of seven, and ultimately majoring in literature in college. Victoria enrolled in law school in 1977 to earn a steady living, thinking she would continue to write as a lawyer. But 12 years into her career as a civil litigator in Southern California, she felt something was missing. Her practice had become all-consuming, and Victoria felt she had lost "whole parts" of herself, as she puts it.

At this key turning point in her life, Victoria decided to enroll in a fiction writing class at UCLA, where she was thrilled to find herself among people who were passionate about the same things as she was. She took four quarters of fiction writing, joined a writers' group, and began writing first poetry and then short fiction for literary journals. "My fiction writing taught me a skill that ultimately put me on the path to blogging—the concept of narrative," Victoria said.

Victoria's legal practice was focused primarily on insurance coverage, antitrust, unfair competition, patent, copyright, and trademark litigation. After nearly 25 years in an adversarial role, she had a keen understanding of what conflict was and how it worked. Finding herself at another turning point, she wanted to transition into a more collaborative role. So, in 2004, Victoria enrolled in the Straus Institute for Dispute Resolution at Pepperdine University School of Law, joined the Southern California Mediation Association, and soon founded Settle It Now Dispute Resolution Services, even before earning her LLM in dispute resolution. Victoria has served as a commercial mediator and arbitrator for the American Arbitration Association in Los Angeles since 2008.

In 2006, Victoria launched a blog focusing on negotiation and mediation, the *Negotiation Law Blog*. Her goal was to present herself as a sophisticated, top-tier commercial negotiator providing resolution of complex commercial disputes. The blog didn't immediately bring in the business she wanted. She came to realize that Am Law 500 firms didn't often hire women mediators. To many, Victoria explained, "mediators were hired to overpower the will of the other side, and when these hiring attorneys envisioned power, they saw a man." Of course, Victoria didn't see it like that, and she believed strongly that gender shouldn't matter. She began writing about unconscious gender bias, and that brought a whole different market to her.

Women began contacting Victoria to ask for advice on salary negotiation, and women's organizations started asking her to present programs teaching negotiation tactics. This was not what she set out to do, but it became apparent that she was writing her way into a new profession, a viable offshoot of her mediation career. While Victoria continued to practice commercial arbitration, in 2010 she and her business partner, Lisa Gates, cofounded She Negotiates Consulting and Training and its corresponding website. For nearly three years, Victoria and Lisa wrote a thrice-weekly negotiation blog at *ForbesWoman*. They currently write a negotiation advice column for popular career blog *The Daily Muse*, a column Victoria began in February of 2012. "When you write," she explains, "you're still learning. Writing allows me to share and to realize my goal of making the lives of lawyers and others happier, and their efforts more efficient."

Eventually, Victoria's *Negotiation Law Blog* did attract the readers she originally had sought, and she became a trusted voice in the mediation community. She began receiving referrals from practicing lawyers also in the blogosphere and started attending conferences to meet with other legal bloggers and deepen the relationships that had begun online. Established legal publications such as the *ABA Journal* interviewed her, not only on mediation topics, but also on the use of social media, which she had been using extensively as a marketing tool.

The idea for Victoria's first book also came to her while blogging. *The Grownups' ABCs of Conflict Resolution*, a humorous but insightful illustrated primer on dealing with difficult people, was published in 2010 and is now in its second edition. Not long after, book publisher John Wiley & Sons sent out a query to mediation bloggers looking for authors. Victoria responded and ended up as coauthor of *Success as a Mediator for Dummies*, a 2012 release in the wildly popular "For Dummies" series.

Victoria recommends that all lawyers find a way to speak and write as part of their business development plan. "If you have a book," she adds, "you'll get the best speaking gigs, with the biggest and swankiest audiences. To land that kind of speaking engagement, you need a book, to prove you can speak as an authority in a field." She has also been interviewed and cited by numerous major media outlets, including CNN, the *Wall Street Journal*, and NPR. She attributes all of it—her successful practice, her consultancy, her books—to that original blog she started back in 2006.

Staci Jennifer Riordan

Partner, Nixon Peabody LLP

Fashion Law

Staci Riordan never considered herself a natural writer and didn't write much of anything until she became a lawyer. She is quick to point out, "I can't spell and I'm dyslexic. I'm more of a numbers person. So it surprised even me when I came to realize as a litigation associate that my favorite thing to write was briefs." Those briefs ended up awakening her to the value of tailoring her writing to her clients.

Staci grew up in the fashion industry, coming from a long line of garment makers, retailers, and wholesalers. Prior to attending law school, she spent eight years as an apparel industry executive, handling branding, sales, hiring, production, operations, supply chain, and imports for a variety of apparel and textile companies. In 1998, Staci began a six-year stint as a professor at the Fashion Institute of Design and Merchandising; she enrolled in law school in 2001, intent on becoming a lawyer to better serve the business needs of fashion industry professionals. Although a fashion law specialty didn't seem to exist at that time, she knew that was what she was going to practice.

When Staci became an associate at her first law firm, she noticed that the lawyers there didn't communicate the way their clients preferred. "Having worked in the fashion industry, I knew how industry insiders talked," Staci explained, "and it wasn't anything like the way attorneys did." Her background informed the way she developed her voice as a lawyer, to the initial dismay of her supervising partners. "I remember working on a lengthy licensing agreement and realizing there was no way the client was going to read through all 48 pages of it," she recounted. "So I developed a cover sheet that summarized the agreement into bullet points. A partner who saw this was horrified, telling me I'd be committing malpractice by doing it this way. But I defended my method, knowing that it would more effectively serve the client."

Staci's tailored communication techniques extended to client meetings as well. "I used the same tone and style as my clients did to get across key messages," she said. "I'd never seen a designer sit through a meeting with a lawyer talking traditional legal-speak for longer than five minutes. You have to approach clients where they are. If they don't understand you, you can't be effective." Her instincts set her on the right path, and she grew her fashion law practice to focus on transactional, commercial, and intellectual property litigation issues faced by manufacturers, retailers, importers, exporters, entertainment entities, and business proprietors.

Within the next few years, Staci stepped up her writing to include client alerts, quarterly articles, program materials, and social media postings, all written in her client-friendly style. In 2009, legal business development coach Cordell Parvin encouraged her to start a blog. With all the writing she was already doing, he pointed out, she might as well pull it together in one place. What's more, her firm at that time, Fox Rothschild, already hosted quite a few attorney blogs. And so Staci's *Fashion Law Blog* was born.

Before she launched her blog, Staci reviewed a large number of legal blogs but found most of them dry. Determined to make hers different, she wrote in a casual, conversational style. Within the first six months after launch, the blog was attracting new clients. "I'd get feedback saying they loved my blog, which they often found in Google search results," Staci said. She has heard from readers who are fashion industry general counsel, designers, manufacturers, and retailers working for companies ranging from start-ups to large publicly owned corporations. Staci started out posting once a week, then eventually shifted to posting once a day for a one-year stretch. With her now-thriving practice, she has dialed back to weekly posts. "I can't recall the last time a new client who contacted me *didn't* find me through my blog," Staci observed.

In addition to potential clients, the blog has attracted numerous inquiries from other attorneys and from law students interested in learning about fashion law. The mounting number of queries prompted Staci to compile a list of FAQs for her readership.

Staci credits her blog for creating additional business development opportunities. "It seems every speaking engagement I've been offered has come about as a result of my blog," she explains. She currently speaks about once a week. The blog also led to an invitation by alma mater Loyola Law School to teach their first-ever course in fashion law. Loyola subsequently asked Staci to help create and direct the Fashion Law Project, a comprehensive academic center focused on the unique legal issues affecting the fashion industry in the United States and worldwide. Staci currently serves as an adjunct professor, teaching fashion law and running the Fashion Law Clinic. In addition, as the Fashion Law Project's executive director, she oversees the annual Fashion Law Symposium and Fashion Law Summer Intensive. Staci is currently writing a casebook for use in fashion law courses.

In October 2014, Staci joined Nixon Peabody as a partner in their intellectual property counseling and transactions practice in the firm's Los Angeles office. There she chairs the fashion law team, and she now blogs at http://staciriordan.com.

As much as she couldn't have dreamed her blog would bring her as far as it has, Staci is adamant that it would never have been successful if she hadn't stayed true to her voice. "The fashion industry is filled with creative people," she explained. "To offer them the sound legal advice they need, I have to write for my audience, using their language. Otherwise, it wouldn't work." Her firm is extremely supportive of her blog, but when she first started out, it was more of a challenge. "My biggest initial challenge was winning over the naysayers who insisted, 'You don't sound like a lawyer; how will you ever attract clients?' But then they saw how good my blog's metrics were, and that was the proof they needed."

Staci's advice to any attorney considering a blog is first and foremost to stay true to oneself: "You can't try to be someone you're not; you have to be authentic. Writing a blog is very personal. Your readers get to know you, and they see you as a friend. That connection is key to keeping them coming back. And you have to know your target audience. If you don't understand who they are, you might not be addressing them in the correct way. Be sure to adjust your tone based on the feedback you receive."

Bloggers will find it easier to come up with ideas for posts if they identify topics they enjoy and then learn as much as they can about them. "Find out who else is writing on the topic," Staci advises. "Figure out how you can approach it differently. Demonstrate your experience, your perspective, and your skills. Give readers a reason to hire you." Finding the time to write is key and, as mentioned earlier, when to do it will vary from person to person. Staci's writing schedule has fluctuated over the years. When she was posting every day, she tended to write mostly at night. Now she writes her posts in batches, sometimes midmorning and other times over an extended lunch break.

Staci also does not believe in delegating blog posts to associates, as some partners do. "Nobody should ever post in your name," Staci emphasized. "You'll lose authenticity if you allow 'ghost posts.' Instead you can ask others to help with research, or have guest contributors post under their own names. But you have to protect your brand."

Carolyn Elefant

Owner and Principal Attorney, Law
Offices of Carolyn Elefant

Energy Law

Carolyn Elefant is likely as well known for her
award-winning and long-running blog, My
Shingle, as she is for her busy energy law practice. Launched in December of 2002, My *Shingle* was the first blog dedicated to serving solo
and small firm lawyers and those who want to start their own practice.

After beginning her legal career with a stint as an attorney advi-
sor to the Federal Energy Regulatory Commission (FERC), Carolyn
worked as an associate at a national energy regulatory law firm for
three and a half years. In November of 1993, she founded her own
firm, which continues to thrive today. Carolyn's practice focuses on
energy regulatory matters, with heavy emphasis on FERC practice
and policy, emerging renewables and smart grid, federal siting and
eminent domain, social media and privacy in the utility industry, and
energy-related litigation and appeals.

Carolyn has always enjoyed writing. She was a principal contributor to her law school newsletter, in fact compiling the newsletter on
her Macintosh computer—likely one of the first in her class to own
a computer at home. Once practicing, she authored law review articles and wrote client updates on the energy industry for her first firm.
After starting her solo practice, Carolyn created a website for her firm
in 1995, a real novelty in those days. As online technology continued
to progress, a blog was the next logical step. "I had been writing about
legal practice on an online portal for a year, and by the time it was
ready to launch, it morphed into a blog," Carolyn explained. With
that, she became a part of a community of early "blawgers" and found
herself connecting with like-minded lawyers across the nation.

A little over a year later, Carolyn created a second blog, this one
focusing on the energy industry, to demonstrate her knowledge and
experience in that area. Eventually, as she began writing more in-
depth articles rather than brief posts, that blog evolved into a newsletter out of necessity. "In addition, many potential clients at larger
firms weren't reading blogs at that time," Carolyn recalled, "so it made
more sense to recast the blog as a newsletter."

For that matter, it took a while for My *Shingle* to build up readership. In its early days, there were as few as 30 followers. That gradually

changed as more lawyers became familiar with this fledgling online medium. Her readership was boosted when Carolyn was invited by Lisa Stone, another early blogger and a cofounder of *BlogHer*, to have *My Shingle* join a network of blogs that were handpicked and aggregated by American Legal Media (ALM). Lisa was also the original author of ALM's *Legal Blog Watch*, a popular blog that rounds up some of the more interesting content from the legal blogosphere. In early 2006, Lisa handed over the reins of *Legal Blog Watch* to Carolyn and to Robert Ambrogi, another highly respected lawyer blogger. From February 2006 through September 2009, Carolyn wrote an average of ten posts a week, roughly 50 weeks a year, for a total of 1,680 posts on *Legal Blog Watch*. Her contributions there raised her profile exponentially.

Although *My Shingle* brought Carolyn a great deal of notoriety as a commentator and champion of solos and small firms, she says it did not necessarily directly generate a lot of new legal work. It did result in many offers of speaking engagements, which strengthened her name recognition and credentials. By 2007 or 2008, her readership was large enough to attract paid sponsors of her blog, and it was then that it began to generate actual revenue, as well as speaking and consulting assignments.

In January of 2008, Carolyn's first book was published by LawyerAvenue Press, *Solo by Choice: How to Be the Lawyer You Always Wanted to Be*. Building on the advice she had shared for years on *My Shingle*, Carolyn created a comprehensive, detailed guide to setting up and maintaining a solo law practice. In 2011, a second edition of the book was released, along with *Solo by Choice, The Companion Guide: 34 Questions That Could Transform Your Legal Career*, in which Carolyn compiled tips and insights from nearly 50 solo lawyers in response to practical questions lawyers should consider when launching their own practices. With the faltering economy, more and more new as well as seasoned lawyers were turning to solo practice, and these books built Carolyn's reputation further and led to yet more speaking opportunities.

As more social media outlets emerged, Carolyn assembled an e-book on social media for her blog. She then found herself speaking more regularly on how to effectively and ethically use social media in a law practice. Following a conversation at ABA TECHSHOW in 2009, a member of the ABA Law Practice Management Section book publishing board approached Carolyn about writing a book on the topic. Carolyn recruited lawyer Nicole Black, who also used social media extensively in her practice, to be her coauthor. The resulting guidebook, *Social Media for Lawyers: The Next Frontier*, was published by the ABA in 2010 to strong reviews. That book in turn led to Carolyn discussing social media issues in the regulatory industry, prompting yet more speaking opportunities. "I didn't intend to set myself out as an authority on social media as a marketing tool," she explains. "Although I can advise lawyers on how to use social media for marketing, I am more comfortable addressing legal questions on topics such as the ethical use of social media by lawyers, or the lawful use of social media in heavily regulated industries like the energy sector."

While Carolyn was doing all this writing and speaking, she continued to maintain and grow her burgeoning energy law practice. In addition to serving a growing client base, in 2005 she cofounded the Ocean Renewable Energy Coalition, the only national trade association exclusively dedicated to promoting marine and hydrokinetic energy technologies from clean, renewable ocean resources. She continues to serve as its general and regulatory counsel.

So when does this busy practitioner and mother of two find time to write? "When my daughters were younger," Carolyn says, "I would do it after they got home from school and were otherwise occupied. I also would work on both my *Above the Law* and *My Shingle* posts on Sundays. Now I post to my blog three mornings a week. Some days I know exactly what I want to write about and it's easy. Other days, it takes longer; maybe a couple of hours. Some posts have a sense of urgency and have to go up on the blog right away. Others can be staggered and scheduled later.

"I go through phases with the writing. When my practice gets extremely busy, it's more difficult to schedule it in. The topics themselves go in cycles; some of them haven't changed over the years and arise periodically."

Carolyn's advice for potential bloggers is straightforward: "First, ask yourself if you really like to write, and if you truly enjoy the topic you've chosen to focus on. If you don't, it's going to be very hard to keep it up. If it feels tortuous to write regularly, you won't succeed. If blogging isn't for you, look to another medium."

If you decide to go forward, "first read other blogs to see what's out there—and what's not," Carolyn advises. "There are bigger gaps in what's being covered than you may think. Take note of the writing style that's used. You'll see the most effective posts are conversational. Learn how to write for your readers. When you first start out, you can blog about what others have said on your topic, quoting them, and then add to the conversation."

Those who don't have the discipline to blog regularly might consider producing a newsletter instead. It can be pushed out via email as well as posted on the firm's website monthly, quarterly, or at whatever interval you choose. Or, a newsletter can be done in addition to a blog. Carolyn includes case summaries and analysis in her newsletter. She also periodically shares a short personal item, which she finds people enjoy.

As a solo, Carolyn is always competing against larger firms, so she has to keep up and continue to demonstrate her skills and experience. Writing consistently for more than a decade has given her the credibility and earned her the credentials she needs to be successful. Although the platforms she uses may very well continue to evolve, she will continue to write in whatever form best serves both her audience and her business goals.

Nicole Black

Lawyer, Author, Director of Business Development and Community Relations at MyCase, Of Counsel, Fiandach & Fiandach

Civil Litigation and Criminal Defense

You can hear a sense of wonder in Nicole Black's voice as she recounts the unexpected turns her career path has taken on the way to where she is now as an attorney, author, analyst, speaker, and business development professional. It was not a path Niki ever considered in her younger years, let alone plotted out, but like many seemingly serendipitous journeys, it has brought her to a place she believes she is meant to be.

After Niki was admitted to the New York State Bar in 1996, she was hired as an assistant public defender in the Monroe County Public Defender's Office, where she worked for nearly four years, handling over 3,000 criminal cases. In 1999, Niki left the Public Defender's Office to work at a midsized civil litigation and criminal defense firm in Rochester. There she continued to handle criminal defense matters, as well as civil litigation cases of all types, and eventually built up her own employment discrimination practice. Despite her success, after four years, Niki felt she wasn't on the right path. "I could feel my creativity shutting down. Among other things, my writing had become so analytical." Despite the fact she was on track to make partner, Niki left the firm.

She stayed home and started a family, but after two and a half years she worried she was becoming too far out of the loop. "I had read that after three years of not practicing law, it would be extremely difficult to find work again," Niki recalled, "so I knew I had to get back into it soon." A self-proclaimed "geek" and early adopter of technology, Niki created a website and prepared to hang out her own shingle to find contract work from other lawyers.

At about the same time, she heard about the new medium known as blogs and decided to start one. She had to demonstrate she was up to date with the law and thought blogging would be a good way to do that. It was then, in November of 2005, that she began her first blog, *Sui Generis*, focusing on New York law. "Since my target audience was New York lawyers, I obviously needed to write about things that would be particularly interesting to them." She reported on criminal defense cases, New York civil procedure, New York court appointments, constitutional issues, and employment and labor law, among many other topics. The blog helped Niki get her name out and establish her credentials, leading to the contract work she had been seeking.

In early 2007, Niki began doing more and more contract work for Fiandach & Fiandach, one of the largest DWI defense firms in New York, and she became of counsel to the firm, a position she still holds today. She continued writing *Sui Generis* and also began writing "Legal Loop," a weekly column for the *Daily Record*, a newspaper based in western New York providing legal, real estate, and business news. Her early columns focused on criminal law and now typically cover topics at the intersection of technology and the law.

Writing has always come easy to Niki, and she has found a variety of outlets to distribute her content. The first book Niki coauthored was *Criminal Law in New York*, a comprehensive legal treatise published by Thomson Reuters that she has updated regularly with coauthor Karen Morris. Niki eventually expanded her blogging to include humorous stories with a legal bent, which became so popular she created a separate blog for them, called *Legal Antics*. She also blogged on issues facing women lawyers, resulting in yet another popular blog titled *Women Lawyers—Back on Track*. After several years, Niki retired both of these offshoot blogs, explaining, "As popular as *Legal*

Antics had become, it didn't lead to any real business connections and didn't forward my goals. And it took up valuable time. My blog for women attorneys served its purpose for a while, but, frankly, it eventually got depressing to write it, and since others were also writing on the topic, it was time to let it go."

Gradually, as Niki's passion for legal technology grew, the focus of her writing changed as well. In 2009 she started yet another blog, *lawtechTalk*, where until 2012 she examined trends in legal technology, with a focus on Internet-based and mobile technologies, the use of smartphones and tablets in legal practice, and the latest developments in social media. Niki began demonstrating and reviewing legal technology tools and products, creating videos in addition to writing. As a result, increasingly more of her speaking engagements focused on legal technology.

Niki became known in the legal industry for her prolific use of social media, including Twitter, where her follower base has grown exponentially. Well-regarded energy lawyer and legal blogger Carolyn Elefant asked Niki to coauthor the ABA book *Social Media for Lawyers: The Last Frontier*, published in 2010. Not long after, Niki pitched a second title to the ABA, *Cloud Computing for Lawyers*, and it was published in 2012, just as the concept of cloud computing was gaining real momentum in the legal industry. Those books heightened her name recognition and brought her yet more high-profile speaking opportunities.

Many news outlets have turned to Niki for commentary and analysis due to her reputation in the legal technology community. She has been widely quoted in numerous bar association and national legal publications, including *Lawyers Weekly* and the *ABA Journal*, as well as in mainstream business publications such as the *Wall Street Journal* and *Forbes*.

In 2011, Niki began her stint as an analyst with Gigaom, an online media company providing news, events, and research on business-related technologies. Then in early 2012, while at the LegalTech New York conference, she met the founders of MyCase, which is web-based practice management software for lawyers. Shortly afterward, she accepted a job with MyCase as their director of business development and community relations. "It's been a great fit for me," Niki explains. "I can work for them and, as part of my job, I am able to continue my writing and speaking." Niki regularly contributes to the MyCase blog, as well as to the *Above the Law* and *Legal IT Professionals* blogs.

Involved in as much as she is, Niki finds herself writing nearly every weekday. She begins many days by reading the latest news and analysis to decide which topics and trends to write about and share on social media. This might take up to two hours, after which she often spends an hour writing. After lunch she usually spends two to three hours writing blog posts and articles, and then for the rest of the afternoon, she answers email, takes phone calls, and works on nonwriting projects. Because Niki is always writing about topics of keen interest to her, it doesn't get old for her. "That's the key," she confirms. "You have to find your passion, something that's not a chore to write about. If you find it tedious, it's going to be painful for you and it's going to be painful for your readers. My best advice to others is to write about things you want to learn about yourself. Find topics that really get you going."

* * *

But Can *You Do It? Yes, You Can!*

Ideally, the stories of how these five women lawyers have successfully leveraged writing in their varied practices will inspire you to do the same in yours. Perhaps those of you who have already done some writing of your own have picked up a few fresh ideas you can try out. But if you haven't used writing as a business development tool before and are still skeptical or unsure that you can make it work for you, let's review some of the advice we've covered and address your concerns.

"I don't know where to start? What do I write about?"

Start by choosing a broad topic, one that is directly related to your practice or your passions and that involves issues affecting the clients you most want to attract. Make a list of those issues or subtopics that could be addressed in an article, writing down as many as you can think of. Highlight those that are the most timely—hot topics—as well as those that are consistently of interest to the clients you are targeting. Then choose the highlighted topics that interest *you* the most, topics that you would enjoy writing about, whether because they are subjects you know inside

> *"Start by choosing a broad topic, one that is directly related to your practice or your passions. . ."*

and out or because they're something you would like to research further. Now you've narrowed it down to the topics to focus on.

"But what if a lot of other lawyers are already writing on my topic?"

Very likely others *will* have written on your topic, but perhaps not as many as you suspect. You need to survey what's already out there, identifying and searching through the periodicals and blogs most likely to address that topic. Much of your research can easily be conducted online.

"I've only done traditional legal writing; how do I make my content more interesting?"

It does take some practice to switch to a different style of writing, but it isn't necessarily difficult. You likely have a few (or several) favorite periodicals and blogs that you enjoy reading regularly. And, as part of your preparation for writing, you're going to be reading additional articles and blog posts on your chosen topic. Pay attention to the writing style you find most appealing, the style that seems most effortless while still being informative. Most likely it will be conversational rather than dry and academic. You'll want to adopt a similar style, one that flows easily while it imparts the intended information. You should be talking *with* your audience, not at them. Inject your personality into your writing to make it your own.

"How will I know I'm on the right track with my 'voice'?"

Once you have established a style that feels comfortable and seems effective, share a partial draft of your piece with a trusted colleague or two. Ask for unfiltered, brutally honest feedback on how it flows, if it's interesting, and if it's instructive. You'll likely get some helpful input on how you might improve it. Once you have a revised draft, go back to those same reviewers for additional feedback to see if you've hit the mark. But also ask one or two other people who can act as representatives of your intended audience to review the piece. These should be people who are interested in the subject matter and would like to learn more about it—not people who are already well versed in the topic. They will be able to give you input not only on your style of writing, but on whether it is accessible and clear enough to be understood by a novice.

With this feedback in hand, you should be able to polish your piece until you are confident that it reflects your unique voice while being informative. As you continue to write, your style will develop further and it will become second nature.

"I'm already too busy with billable work. How will I ever find the time for this?"

Please refer back to the discussion on scheduling at the start of this chapter. You don't need to write every day the way some of the women profiled here do. The important thing is to get started. Schedule a couple hours the first week and see how much you get accomplished. And don't give up too easily! Think of it the way you do when establishing any new routine, be it exercising or adapting to a new commute. It takes a while to get into the groove, but eventually the new activity becomes integrated into your schedule. Once you begin making real progress, you'll find the enthusiasm and motivation to continue.

Yes, You Can Do It

Just remember celebrated writer Isabel Allende's words of wisdom: "Show up, show up, show up, and after a while the muse shows up, too."

Chapter 6

Speaking

Carol Schiro Greenwald

People often fear public speaking more than facing a tiger in the jungle. But if you aren't afraid of tigers or audiences, you may want to know how these women lawyers used speech-making strategies to gain visibility, professional respect, career advancement, and clients. For the women profiled here, speaking engagements are a natural extension of their networking activities—a chance to show their leadership qualities and substantive knowledge. They view it as a way to show others not only what they think but how they think, which gives potential buyers a chance to visualize how it would be to work with them.

Advantages of Speech Making as a Business Technique

- Speaking is a core lawyer capability.
- Speaking outside the legal system uses the same technique for different purposes.
- Public speaking develops poise and confidence.
- A speech allows an audience to see you in action—how you speak, how you think, how you relate to others.
- You are seen as the expert.
- Twenty-first-century prospects want to "touch and feel" before they purchase. Q&A time lets them do this.
- Once you learn to love it, by communicating this feeling, you present yourself in a positive light.
- Speaking provides myriad opportunities to begin new relationships.

Why Speaking Engagements Make Rain

Speeches are an excellent way to get face time in front of colleagues, clients, and prospects in a professional manner that showcases your knowledge. Each speech before a well-chosen audience provides four kinds of advantages:

1. *Personal brand platform:* The speaker reinforces her personal brand as an expert in specific legal fields and client industries—the first step in a sales cycle based on establishing trust.

2. *Business development:* Attendees' personal impressions of the speaker grow as they listen to a speech on a relevant topic in an environment they already trust. When they ask questions and receive personal replies, the interaction suggests how the speaker works as a professional.

3. *Marketing:* The speaker and her firm gain visibility before these audiences because she will be listed in all marketing materials from the host organization. This kind of "third party" endorsement is crucial in creating external recognition for the speaker and validating her expertise.

4. *Public relations:* Often vertical press representatives attend such events, and may quote the speaker in subsequent articles.

The Speaker's Game Plan

To use speeches as a business development tool requires forethought, planning, and a willingness to spend time before and after the event. It begins with planning to identify the kinds of people the person wants to meet. The next step is to find audiences that include these kinds of people. Speakers need to research possible opportunities and identify places to contact for speaking opportunities. Once these are selected, the speaker should research the audience in order to customize her talk to their interests and concerns.

At the event, the speaker needs to arrive early and stay late in order to connect with her audience on a one-to-one basis. Asking the audience if they would like to receive more information on her topic through firm newsletters or blogs and exchanging business cards with interested audience members are two additional techniques for extending the speaking experience into the sales cycle.

Once home from the event, speakers should connect on LinkedIn with audience members who have given them their business cards or through specific emails to all those who have chosen to request a subsequent relationship. Those names should also be added to the speaker's contact list.

By following these steps, speakers can show audiences how their expertise connects with the audiences' needs and use this connection as the jumping-off point for developing relationships.

Five Women Who Did It

None of the women profiled for this chapter has had professional training in public speaking. All came to it more or less naturally as they sought ways to connect with clients and prospects. All found that they really love public speaking because it gives them an opportunity to share their knowledge through interactions with their audiences. The speaking process becomes the beginning of an association that leads to a relationship, and often to work.

Each of these women attributes her career successes to the visibility speaking gave her, which in turn led to new clients and add-on work for current clients. The three lawyers in private practice all see a close relationship between success as a public speaker, their partnership status, and their standing within their firms.

Figure 6.1. Speaking Strategy and Process Cycle

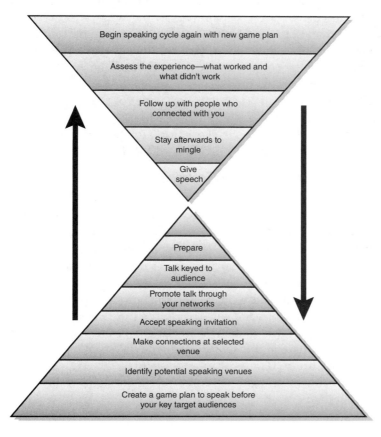

Tara C. Fappiano

Partner, Havkins Rosenfeld Ritzert
& Varriale, LLP

Insurance Defense Litigation

Tara Fappiano is the resident partner in the White Plains, New York, office of Havkins Rosenfeld Ritzert & Varriale, LLP, a medium-sized, New York insurance defense firm. She is a vibrant, outgoing, engaging professional with a beautiful smile that brings you right into her circle. She is also a tough litigator who handles the full range of insurance defense cases, with a special focus on toxic tort and environmental issues. In addition, she counsels businesses regarding environmental claims management and employee compliance issues.

And, she is a wife and mother, active in her children's school activities. She is cochair of two committees for the Westchester County Bar Association and chair of the Special Education Parent/Teacher Association for the Tuckahoe Union Free School District. For several years she wrote a regular column in the Westchester Women's Bar Association newsletter.

She has also been a moot court judge for the Pace University School of Law National Environmental Moot Court Competition, the American Bar Association Negotiation Competition, and the New York State Bar Association High School Mock Trial Tournament.

Career-building through Public Speaking

Tara began her career at Orhenstein & Brown, rising from associate to counsel. In 2007 her group decided to split and form their own firm. She went with them. Her first office was in an executive suite; today the firm has their own Westchester office. In the beginning, as the resident—and only—partner, she struggled, overwhelmed with administrative duties.

Her first priority was to make her firm's office in this new location both visible and viable. She says that at the time she knew a bit about supervising, but nothing about marketing. Her only previous experience was in amateur theater. Her first public speaking opportunity was as a panelist on CLE programs for clients.

She began by integrating three techniques she thought would bring visibility:

1. *Writing:* She began a column in the Westchester Women's Bar Association newsletter titled "Parenting for Professionals," dealing with the complex issues that face working attorneys raising families.
2. *Cold/warm calling:* She Googled prospects pursuing opportunities to provide in-house CLE for their adjusters. She revved up her own contact list, seeking referrals and reconnecting with people as they moved from one company to another. As she says, "I worked my relationships."
3. *Public speaking:* She would say, "I can speak on [timely topic], or if you want something else, I'd be glad to do that instead." Then she would provide examples of topical subjects, such as lead paint liability, social media discovery, and changes in civil procedure rules.

These tri-part techniques continue, and continue to work. Today her office consists of one counsel, two associates, several paralegals, and law school interns, plus support staff. Tara has spent considerable time refining the legal process she follows in order to be able to pitch for and handle caseload volume in a cost-effective way. She says that the pressure to be cost-competitive "intensified with the advent of electronic billing and then increased due to the impact of the 2008 recession."

Sharing Knowledge Brings in Work

Tara says that her most effective sales technique is to hold CLEs for claim agents, lawyers, and adjusters, either clients or prospects, at their offices. She says, "This is the most effective and direct way to market. No one eats out anymore. But when you go to them and provide an interesting talk with CLE credits while they eat a lunch I pay for, it's a win-win—I get to spend time with them and they get to see how I present myself professionally and how I think about their issues." She keys her talks to topics that will help them with their everyday work responsibilities such as the latest trends in New York State law.

In the beginning, she would pick up the phone and call past clients or warm prospects to offer this freebie. Today most of these opportunities result from companies' invitations. For example, she went to the Midwest to present a CLE session to a client who had given her firm a couple of conflict cases. She came back with more work, "because they had met us." Most of these excursions are to out-of-state insurance offices. This exposure leads to work when the client they visited has a

New York case. As Tara says, "I'm always happy to be second choice or local counsel."

She uses e-blasts to her client list to share important decisions and supplement the quarterly firm newsletter that goes to everyone on the firm mailing list. The firm also helps by providing a culture that encourages and supports time to learn and use business development skills.

Working Her Relationships

At first Tara pursued everyone and anyone she knew. She would Google acquaintances and send them emails. She followed people as they moved from company to company. She would ask clients for referrals and follow up. Her success rate was about one opportunity from 20 calls. Today she uses LinkedIn to find and build relationships. "I look for old contacts and follow them, or new people in places with new business, or review the contacts of colleagues on LinkedIn to see who knows whom and ask for introductions."

Fitting in Marketing

How does she do it all—run an office, serve as chief client relationship partner, litigate cases, and be the office rainmaker? By working smarter. She tries to reuse any written piece or PowerPoint so that for new events it only takes three to four hours to update cases and prepare her speech. Her speaking schedule continues at a more moderate pace, with two to three in-house CLEs per year, one or two bar association CLEs, and one or two talks in her firm's lecture series. Tara does most of the work, such as finding speaking venues, herself. She typically spends one day a month doing only marketing and another few hours weekly, usually during lunch time.

Networking

Thinking back to the three techniques Tara uses—writing, cold/warm calling, and public speaking—notice that there are no networking luncheons. Why not? Tara says, "Because I hate cocktail chit-chat. I find it hard to sell myself that way, but give me knowledge I can share—and I am very comfortable." Like most successful rainmakers, Tara emphasizes those techniques that put her in situations where she feels comfortable.

Why It Works

Tara's techniques work because they give her face time (or on-the-phone voice connections) with prospects and clients. It allows her to communicate. As she says, "I share my value with them and they decide if it is worth it or not. People give business to people they like, but first you need to establish your credentials in order to be considered."

> *"Speaking as the expert puts me in a position of authority and shows off my intelligence."*

Is It Worth It?

Tara says absolutely. She enumerates the following reasons:

1. "Speaking shows people who you are and provides an opportunity for you to ask about them."
2. "Speaking is a very good form of differentiation for a woman. It allows me to show what I have to offer and to establish my credentials. Speaking as the expert puts me in a position of authority and shows off my intelligence. It provides a platform for respect."
3. Approximately one quarter of her revenue comes from contacts met through speaking engagements. Her book of business supports the Westchester office of her firm.

But equally important to Tara, speaking is the foundation for rising respect and stature within her own firm. Her voice is considered more seriously because she is a rainmaker—she is a player.

Asked what the impact of her own book of business has had on her career, she says, "It has made every difference."

Amy B. Goldsmith

Partner, Tarter Krinsky & Drogin LLP
Intellectual Property

Amy Goldsmith is a petite, intense, curly-haired dynamo who conveys her passion for her work in everything she does. As an intellectual property attorney, she focuses on the connections between the global interests of her clients and the role patents play in their international strategy. Her energy, intelligence, and concern for clients come through naturally in her public speaking.

Doing What Comes Naturally

Asked how she came to public speaking as a way to build her book of business, she says it came naturally. Even before law school, her college sorority encouraged her to run for the Cornell Campus Council. During the next three years, actively involved in campus governance, she became used to public speaking and found she liked it. As she says, "So I went to law school."

She joined Gottlieb, Rackman & Reisman, PC, an intellectual property boutique, right out of law school and stayed there for the next 26 years. Looking for public speaking opportunities as an associate, she taught an intellectual property course at a local law school.

In the 1990s, Amy started to approach business development in a more formal and strategic way. For many reasons, including a lack of firm travel funds, she needed to concentrate on New York City opportunities, so her initial focus became the fashion industry. Time spent at events such as the Javits Center jewelry trade show established what has become her personal marketing approach:

1. Combining public speaking, in-person networking, and a social media presence
2. Focusing on venues where she can demonstrate how she uses her patent law knowledge to support her clients' business strategies
3. Building a visibility platform, online and in-person

These techniques lead to opportunities for leadership positions in professional associations, nonprofit organizations, and marketing-oriented groups, which in turn creates more public speaking opportunities. The result of these outreach strategies has been a growing client roster.

In 2012, Amy moved to Tarter Krinsky & Drogin, LLP, a midsize, full-service firm strongly committed to marketing. Her years spent building public awareness and credibility through public speaking began to pay off in new work directly attributable to specific speaking engagements. For example,

1. Amy lectures for Lawline.com, an online provider of CLE for lawyers, which has increased her public credibility as an expert in her field. Several solo practitioners, viewing her as the expert, referred large cases to her that had outgrown their independent capabilities.

2. After a 2013 TEDx talk on a recent Supreme Court decision concerning gene patents, an audience member transferred an ongoing litigation to her.

3. She put together a Lawline.com program that illustrated her approach to cross-selling services. Called "Business in a Box," it brought together lawyers from seven different practice areas who worked through a fictional scenario showing how each of their areas of expertise contributed to the final result.

Marketing through organizations and speeches has become an important source of visibility, recognition of her expertise and authenticity, and clients. She doesn't track the amount of business that comes from speaking activities, but she knows that it is a key to her book of business, which in turn has enabled her to succeed in her career. "You can't get anywhere in today's environment unless you can originate your own clients. Public speaking and networking skills enabled me to be portable. My book of business demonstrates my market power and the results of such skills."

Symbiosis: Public Speaking and Organization Leadership

Her organizational leadership positions cover the gamut from networking to professional and "feel good." Currently her activities revolve around the following groups:

1. Vistage, a networking group that brings together executives from a wide variety of industries for monthly meetings focused on helping members work through strategic and operational issues. Amy's talk to these C-suite executives on intellectual property law led directly to new business.

2. Savvy Ladies, a not-for-profit whose mission is to educate women to become financially savvy, where her role as a member of the executive committee has generated relationships resulting in legal work for her.

3. The New York State Women's Bar Association, for which Amy chairs the CLE program committee, and the local New York City chapter, where she serves as recording secretary; both provide access to other experts, increase her visibility, and create relationships that lead to resources for her own clients.

4. Women in International Trade, where her role as a board member has led to speaking engagements.

All of these groups reflect her personal belief in the organization's mission or provide support for women in terms of their careers and personal growth.

How Does She Do It?

The leadership of her current firm values her contribution to their public image. She typically makes four to six major speeches a year. To prepare new, current, topical talks:

1. Interns conduct research on cutting-edge topics and trends, such as Monsanto patents' consequences in real life;
2. The marketing department prepares her slide deck and prepares news releases about upcoming speeches to circulate to the firm's client list; and
3. Marketing budget funds pay transportation and other associated expenses.

The Value of Public Speaking

She loves it! Amy loves the interaction with audiences, seeing faces as they react to what she says and being able to establish immediate connections when she answers their questions. She says speaking makes connections with potential clients. "Speaking makes me human. It lets a prospect feel as if they already know me based on lectures they've seen."

Amy thinks that in the digital age it is imperative to use social media. Younger people assume everyone will use it. Clients usually use it to prequalify professionals. This is especially true for lawyers and others whose business is referral based. She sees online speeches—videos, webinars, and so on—as a way to "humanize" herself and differentiate her practice from negative lawyer stereotypes. In terms of her relationship with other lawyers, public speaking becomes an indicator of her willingness to do more as well as a credibility and expertise builder.

She typically spends six to eight hours a week on marketing, primarily time cut out from her personal weekend family time. But she sees this as time well spent. Her advice to other women lawyers: "Success as a public speaker helps me feel more confident. I tell other young lawyers that it is important to learn to be comfortable speaking in public. Ask your firm to help you with presentation skills training, finding speaking opportunities, and publicizing these activities."

> ## How to Overcome Speaker Angst
>
> 1. Think of the audience as individuals interested in what you have to say.
> 2. In your mind, see yourself as talking to one or two of them.
> 3. Practice, practice, practice.
> 4. Take three deep, calming breaths before you go onstage.

Nancy B. Schess

Partner, Klein Zelman Rothermel
Jacobs & Schess LLP

*Labor and Employment Law Representing
Management*

Nancy Schess is the consummate networker and public speaker. She is always a charming, concerned host, ready with a quick smile and an engaged approach. Her work requires sound legal expertise and excellent public speaking skills, whether for client training programs, public seminars, or meetings she chairs. Nancy practices labor and employment law representing management. She advises and counsels clients to develop preventive policies and strategies to maximize the company's investment in their personnel assets.

Nancy feels that "public speaking is one of the most valuable tools to learn because it is essentially a communication tool, and the power of communication is indisputable." It is her favorite activity, even though before every speech there is a moment of fear. She says, "That initial prickle of fear charges me up."

She focused mainly on client training during the 1990s. Speaking before outside audiences began just after she made partner. The firm held a round-table seminar on independent contractors and she was one of the speakers. She remembers "the charge I felt as I saw 40 people in the audience listening to me and engaged in what I was talking about." Client training workshops are important aspects of client retention. Public speaking leads to new referral sources and new work.

Nancy divides speaking engagements into two categories: in front of a public audience or client training seminars in clients' offices. Public audiences are found at association meetings and other networking venues. Nancy has spoken at many such meetings, where the activities are a combination of speaking plus networking before and after the speech. She prefers small to midsize events because "I want to see the audience's reaction." For her, large events are too impersonal, and webinars are "odd" because typically there is no visible audience.

Client training seminars are one of her core practice capabilities. She develops and delivers customized training programs on topics such as prevention of workplace harassment, social media in the workplace, effective performance management techniques, and methodologies for dealing with compliance issues. In this kind of situation, her talks are usually quite substantive and her audience very engaged.

Turning Talk into Work

Work often comes—but not necessarily right away. Nancy remembered one instance when she was hired immediately after her speech ended. A woman ran up to her as the session ended and said she had just had a discrimination charge filed against her company. Nancy was hired. Usually it takes longer.

Nancy views public speaking engagements as "opportunities to plant seeds." For example, two years after an American Institute of CPAs (AICPA) speech, an audience member contacted her. The issue fell into her partner's area of expertise. Nancy called the partner, who was away on vacation. The partner responded immediately and won a new client. Another time she spoke at a small round-table session for hospitality industry clients. Two years later, one of them became a client. Why? Nancy attributes the sequence to "having made a connection that the person remembered."

Nancy views the time lag between the speech and the sale as natural because she needs to convince management that prevention pays: "My selling process can take years." For example, she spoke on social media issues at a Society for Human Resource Management (SHRM) meeting attended by human resource professionals. Months later at a networking event, she reconnected with someone who had heard her talk at that meeting. She added the person to her newsletter mailing list. Months passed, and then the woman called to discuss a training program.

Like the other lawyers in private practice, Nancy doesn't track results from her speaking engagements. But she estimates that 15 percent of new clients began as audience members.

It's All about Connecting

Nancy views public speaking and networking as two sides of the same coin. She seeks opportunities to network with audience members. To this end, she employs a couple of strategies.

1. *Follow-up:* She asks for audience contact lists. She also gives out a fax-back sheet asking audience members to sign up for the firm's newsletter. She adds these people to her mailing list. In addition, she adds anyone she speaks with before or after her speech.

2. *Audience selection:* Often people who know of her expertise ask her to speak. But she grew her hospitality industry niche by intentionally focusing on speaking to them wherever possible. She told everyone about this focus, which led to connections that led to speaking opportunities.

She is always looking for connections. Public speaking and networking are two sides of the same business development approach for someone whose goal is to meet and then meet again. To make connections, she tells stories. As she says, "I like to tell stories. There is no absolute right or wrong answer in my practice. So I tell true stories to connect the audience to the issues and my practice strengths."

Nancy spends approximately one-third of her time on marketing activities. The firm provides tremendous support because she does most of the firm's outreach, and they all recognize the need for it. Typically, she spends three to five hours updating and reworking old speeches. New topics take three days to turn into a speech because she needs to gather materials, identify key points that are relevant to her audience, craft the talk, and practice it.

The Significance of Public Speaking for Her Career

Nancy calls the impact of public speaking on her career "significant." She ties it to her promotion to partner and now name partner. Nancy "loves marketing," and public speaking and networking are her favorite techniques.

Allison C. Shields

President, Legal*ease* Consulting Inc.

Law Practice Management and Business Development

Allison Shields is a smart, experienced lawyer who now works with other lawyers to improve their work life through the application of modern practice management techniques and business development skills. As the administrative partner in her law firm, she wore three hats: management, marketing, and legal practice. Overwhelmed and burned out, "a victim of lawyer meltdown," she left legal practice and founded her consultancy in order to "prevent the defection of good lawyers from the profession."

In her prior life as a practicing attorney and administrative partner, she did most of the marketing, but speaking was not a key component of her marketing mix. While she had often shared her ideas through writing articles, speaking seemed so much harder because "you literally had to get in front of people."

She began her consulting practice while winding down her legal practice. Her practice is built on her knowledge of practice management and business development because she sees these areas as key to developing both enjoyable personal practices and a more pleasant firm culture. As an associate, Allison had never been taught these topics, which she terms a gap in her education, and she doesn't want "others to make the same mistake as me." In addition, building her practice around common lawyer experiences gives her a "been there, done that" credibility.

Becoming Comfortable with Public Speaking

Starting over in a whole new context, as a consultant to lawyers, she knew she had to get in front of potential clients. She began in comfortable places with people she knew:

1. In court, with other women lawyers who were waiting with her
2. An executive suite of offices where she knew the owner
3. A local bar association's women lawyers' committee
4. The Suffolk Bar Association Academy of Law, where she volunteered to moderate or speak on programs

Two of her first long-term clients grew out of these initiatives.

For her, the best audience is one where the attendees recognize the importance of marketing and see the connection between practice management, work flow, and productivity. She looks for a mindset—for lawyers ready to make a change.

The Advantages of Speaking In Person

Allison sees speaking to live audiences as a chance to create a chemistry with them that becomes the foundation for trust. She tells stories, often embarrassing ones about herself, as a way of bonding with audiences. She says, "Eye contact is especially important because it helps you make a more personal connection."

She adds, "Speaking provides a great opportunity to make a different kind of connection with people, to demonstrate what you know and to show your personality. Audiences are rooting for you. They are there to learn, and they want you to do well. It's not important to be perfect, just genuine."

Today Allison gives two or three speeches or webinars a month, often paid speeches or speeches tied in to opportunities to sell her books. Even after nine years, though she is very comfortable as a public speaker, she still gets nervous before a speech, wondering, "Am I qualified?" She handles being nervous "by accepting it and seeing the opportunity as a way to stretch my comfort zone." Her reward: "I always feel good when I finish. I always get something positive from the audience."

Allison never had formal marketing training. Initially, she learned from marketing professionals working with her firm and from friends in the business. Asked how much of her work comes from speeches, she says she never segments it out because a speech is just one of the multiple touches needed before making the sale. Allison feels that when seeking clients, "people give up too easily. The timing may be off. Your speech may not coincide with their need for your services." Asked to estimate the amount of time she spends on marketing activities, she estimated one-third of her time, but qualified this by saying, "It is hard to separate marketing and work. I try to repurpose marketing pieces for clients or vice versa."

She calls follow-up "essential." Her follow-up comes in the form of blog posts, newsletters, other writings, and, of course, her speeches, which provide constant touches with those she wants to follow up with. Her website is very visitor oriented. Written in conversational English, it lays out her products and services coupled with opportunities to "sample them online." She also benefits from the assumption of expertise that comes from her books for the ABA Law Practice Division: *Facebook in One Hour for Lawyers* and *LinkedIn in One Hour for Lawyers*. Her website provides direct access for those who want to buy them, and the books are often available for sale at her speaking engagements.

Her advice to other women lawyers: "Just try it. Begin small."

Lisa Solomon

Freelance Lawyer

Legal Research and Writing

Lisa Solomon worked in a small civil litigation firm and as a Lexis-Nexis education specialist before hanging up her own shingle in 1995, three years after graduating from NYU School of Law.

Currently her practice has three facets:

1. Legal Research & Writing is a solo practice focused on legal research and writing services with expertise in drafting and arguing appeals and substantive motions; Lisa is the owner.
2. Legal Research & Writing Pro is focused on helping contract attorneys begin and run successful practices. These services are provided via live and recorded webinars, e-books and/or private coaching. Lisa is the owner.
3. The Billable Hour Company is an online company that sells humorous gifts and greeting cards for lawyers and legal professionals. Lisa is a partner.

She has built her personal brand, which fuels all three of her endeavors through a sophisticated strategy integrating public speaking, writing, association memberships, networking, and public relations. Lisa is a petite dynamo—always enthusiastic, often spunky, constantly inventive, and an excellent lawyer. Her strong entrepreneurial bent and willingness to help others are the foundation of her practice and her approach.

For Lisa, rainmaking means connecting with other lawyers—primarily solos or lawyers in smaller firms. Initially she would speak before groups she belonged to, such as the Westchester Women's Bar Association, the Westchester County Bar Association, and the Women's Bar Association of the State of New York. Her topics focused around better approaches to appeals brief writing so that the briefs stood out as memorable. Today, she also speaks on other aspects of legal writing, best practices, ethics related to working with freelance lawyers, and marketing using blogging and social media.

Working Her Strategy

Lisa's goal is "to be findable as a speaker, writer, and thought leader." Public speaking is her primary business development technique. For her, it comes in several forms:

1. *Creating her own speaking opportunity:* In 2010, Lisa wanted to offer a conference for solos and small firm lawyers. So she did research to find contacts, emailed an invitation, and held the conference for a small audience. Financial result: half a dozen new engagements.

2. *Speaking engagements at bar associations or lawyer networking groups:* Usually someone who has heard her speak or a colleague invites her to participate in a conference or seminar. Financial result: approximately 10 percent of her engagements result from these speeches.

    Often her integrated strategy produces interesting results, as was the case when the Wisconsin Bar Association invited her to pinch-hit for a speaker who cancelled. The association found her through a web search because she was a follower of the original speaker's blog.

3. *Webinars:* Sometimes Lisa hosts her own webinars. Other times she asks colleagues if she can copresent on their webinars. She finds guest opportunities by researching for appropriate audiences, and then asks if she may participate. She follows up, often offering a "freebie" in return for the visibility opportunity.

4. *CLE providers:* Lisa has courses available on Lawline.com: two on legal writing and one on working with contract attorneys. She likes Lawline.com for its scope of offerings and also because the company holds events for speakers, which enables Lisa to expand her network.

Activities that Support the Speech Initiative

Lisa uses her website, www.questionoflaw.net, as a marketing and sales tool. Her site features a list of services buttressed by reasons for outsourcing and outsourcing to her. Client testimonials line both sides of her site. Google Lisa and 39,100 results show up. She shows over 500 connections on LinkedIn.

On her speaking engagements page, she lists not only speech title, locale, and date but also a précis of the topic, plus video testimonials and clips of her speeches. Viewers on her site learn not only where she has spoken but how she sounds and what audience members say about her, thereby tying together snatches of real-life experience with two sources of third-party endorsement—the speech location and audience testimonials.

Her approach to each speaking engagement incorporates classic marketing techniques:

1. *Before an event:* She promotes it on her website, through her Twitter and Facebook accounts, and in her email newsletter. She also checks out other speakers' backgrounds and may connect with them prior to the event.
2. *At the event:* She plans to attend the entire conference to mine its networking potential. She will often appear on multiple panels at the same event.
3. *After the event:* To encourage post-event connections, she follows author/consultant Ari Kaplan's advice and puts a brightly colored flyer on all the seats with an offer for a free giveaway. Kaplan calls this the "principle of reciprocity." She collects the completed forms at the end of her talk and adds the names to her newsletter mailing list.
4. *Reusing materials:* Lisa usually turns speeches into articles, following the marketing maxim to reuse the same material in different ways.

Why Does She Do It?

Lisa says, "Communicating my passion is best expressed through speeches. It comes through in a way not possible through articles." For Lisa, marketing "is not a scheduled activity. It is an always present, ongoing, interwoven part of my day."

Advice for Others

Lisa suggests that those who want to add speaking to their marketing mix should do the following:

1. Put yourself out there as someone who is available and has something interesting to say.
2. Understand that organizations are hungry for real, substantive content.
3. Follow up, follow up, follow up.
4. Give prospects a reason to stay in touch.

Take-aways

These women are amazingly similar. All five are optimistic, active, intelligent, interesting, energetic lawyers who have mastered the art of communicating their enthusiasm and expertise through personal connections with others—using speaking engagements.

None of these women had formal training, but learned public speaking on the job, adapting their ability to talk to people into a proficiency in public speaking. All are in it for the connections, the chance to be real, and the opportunity to show what they know and how they think to people who are potentially interested in working with them.

All five admit to some nervousness before a speech, but see this as an asset, not a liability. All see speaking as one arrow in a quiver of arrows, reinforced by networking, writing, and one-on-one follow-up. All of them love this form of communication and urge every reader of their stories to try it themselves.

Tips from These Women Lawyers

Personal and career advantages of public speaking:

- Speaking gives you the personal authority that comes from demonstrating intelligence and expertise.
- You can differentiate yourself by showing what you have to offer through what you say.
- The content of a speech shows people who you are and suggests how you would be to work with.
- People take you more seriously because being a speaker assumes expertise and provides credibility.
- Business development is a numbers game. Creating new relationships with people in your audiences leads to work.
- A personal book of business is an essential precondition for partnership and partner power.
- Public speaking becomes a fun vehicle for connecting with people.

1. How to Begin
   - Take lessons.
   - Figure out a style that is comfortable for you.
   - Key work-related speeches to your business-growth strategy.
   - Begin with a small audience.
   - Ask colleagues and referral sources to help you find speaking opportunities.
2. Encouragement
   - Don't be afraid.
   - Be patient.
   - Build on small successes.
   - Find the fun in it.
3. Just do it.

Chapter 7

Personal Branding

Katy Goshtasbi

Stop and consider how many things you juggle and manage in a typical day. Let's see, there are the kids, spouse/significant other, family, friends, and, let's not forget—the ever-present career as a woman lawyer. Ever wondered how it is that you manage it all and not leave everyone around you thinking you are rushed, crazed, and taking on too much?

What perception do you leave as a woman lawyer and expert in your field? You may be thinking that you have never even stopped to consider this question because you are too busy working and juggling everything. That is not only fair; it is the point of this chapter.

As women lawyers, we tend to internalize the stress of our to-do lists—and it shows! We run around even more than our male counterparts trying to do it all, taking care of the home front *and* being lawyers. When we take on the role of rainmaker, we are trying to accomplish even more. As a result, we may find ourselves turning blindly in circles regarding marketing, business development, and brand management. We aspire to do it all—yesterday. What's a professional woman to do if she wants to do it all well and not be perceived as anything less than great?!

The solution is to pause and recognize the challenge, focus on your personal brand, and make it a priority, or an "intentional brand." Personal branding is still widely misunderstood. Most lawyers and other professionals think the concept of personal branding centers on developing legal practice logos, graphics, and colors for your banners and websites. Nothing could be further from the truth.

Your personal brand as a lawyer is developed long before your logo, colors, fonts, typeface, or stationery are ever developed. Your personal brand as a female lawyer is all about your uniqueness. After all, you are marketing *you!*

Women are hardwired to advocate and promote others first, often before themselves. Personal brand management will teach you to own your best qualities and develop the discipline to appropriately "toot your own horn"—as a woman and as a fantastic lawyer.

Many people have a poor perception of lawyers. The word *poor* here implies both negative and inaccurate. People wrongly believe lawyers are greedy and bill too much. They also may believe we are arrogant. Hence, the large universe of lawyer jokes out there. Better attention to personal branding can help improve these perception problems.

Even though you are practicing law, you are running a business of practicing law. Even if you think you are not responsible for attracting new business or running the legal business, you are indeed. There is no better path to improve your legal business than by having an *intention* or plan to implement to get there. This same intention then turns into an intentional brand based on self-discovery and genuine, yet calculated, dissemination.

Personal brand development and management is meaningful work and by no means "fluff." Those who avoid working on their personal brand need to be educated about its proper place in the practice management toolbox. As you read on, the goal is to realize that personal branding is a necessary element of your business and career development *and* your development as a person. As well as your practice is doing, it can always be better. Just because we as lawyers are trained to follow precedent, this does not mean you want to do the same in connection with your personal brand development and management by doing what has been done in the past.

This chapter is intended to provide you an overview and a running start on what it means to have an intentional personal brand that opens the door for you to be a great lawyer by being happier, healthier, and more intentionally balanced in your personal and professional life. Keep in mind that none of this happens overnight. There is no need to panic and think you have fallen behind. The materials discussed in this chapter have been developed over many years of running a personal branding company—as a lawyer and for lawyers. Developing and building a personal brand is a journey, not a destination. Increasing your self-awareness and taking steps along the way will take you where you want to go—to creating the career and life of your dreams by carving out your own unique path.

As you read the women profiled in this chapter, learn from their experience and take away nuggets that may work for you. But please don't imitate them. Through their examples, recognize that everyone has a unique path to success as a rainmaker.

As successful professional women, we also have the tendency to want to do it all by ourselves. Developing your personal brand is not a solitary venture. There are professionals who guide and work alongside lawyers to help them build brands that are effective. Consider seeking them out for guidance and support after doing your due diligence into their background, beliefs, and experiences.

Personal Branding Defined

I have developed the following three-part definition of personal branding because over the years I have found it captures the essence of the subject matter well:

1. Identify the essence of your relevant attributes—that is, document your uniqueness.
2. Consistently communicate the essence of your relevant attributes to your audience (i.e., target market or prospects).
3. Learn and interpret how the audience perceives your brand message.

The first part of the definition simply means that people want to know you as a person and decide your brand quality from that perspective—*who you are, not what you do.* So, cultivate a rapport with your targeted audiences and resonate an intentional brand.

The second part of the definition is all about marketing. Yes, marketing. This is where the two Cs come into play—*clarity* and *consistency*—as a must for marketing and branding.

You must be clear about your personal brand: that is, who you are, why you do what you do, and for whom you do it. If you are not clear about your personal brand, no one else can be clear about you and/or your business. That is why I speak of having an intentional brand. You need clarity to have an effective and quality personal brand.

Consistency is about ensuring that your personal and business brand are impressing your target audience with the same message each time you touch them. Consistent communication is the hallmark of any relevant brand, including yours. Consistency presumes you know your target market and audience. Knowing your target market and audience helps you produce a brand that consistently appeals to them and attracts them to you and your business and/or career.

If your brand messaging is not clear and consistent, you run the risk of confusing your audience. Your audience should never mistake you for another lawyer. Instead, clear and consistent communication of your brand should create the feeling that your audience is familiar with you and knows and trusts who you are and what you are about, personally and professionally.

Out of this three-part definition, the part that has the potential to pack the most punch with the most impact is the final part regarding audience perception. Let's be clear: your personal brand is formed by others' perceptions of you.

Personal Branding and Marketing— One and the Same?

Although the topic of personal brand management has become well recognized and an integral part of building a prosperous practice, there is still confusion over how to compare and contrast it with marketing and business development.

Personal branding is a subset of marketing. As noted above, you must market yourself based on your personal brand before you can market your legal practice. Your personal brand is based on your substantive work and our perception of you. Thus, you must have a solid personal brand in order to market and develop your business well.

With respect to sales, personal branding is owning who you are in order to more effectively promote yourself and your legal services. Sales can be defined as a two-way communication between two people—the seller and the prospective buyer. As lawyers, many of us do not like to be sold to because of the possible suspicion people are trying to take advantage of us. If this is your perspective, it may hinder your ability to appropriately position yourself to promote your services. Many people tend to sell with the same mentality that they buy. So if it takes you much mulling over, possible skepticism, and agonizing in order to "buy," then you likely will expect your prospects to not buy "you" easily either, resulting in extending the sales cycle of your rainmaking efforts. The result: slow or no new clients.

Self-Confidence and Self-Promotion

By nature, women tend to be more collaborative, while men are more naturally competitive. This natural lack of drive to compete tends to manifest itself as women lawyers lacking the self-confidence to own their personal brands. With some work, the goal is to develop the self-confidence to toot our own horns, own our successes, self-promote, and be rainmakers.

Everyone has self-confidence issues. Over the years, I have found a direct inverse correlation between stress, self-confidence, and the strength and quality of personal brand management. By extrapolation, your business brand and success in business and career suffer when your personal brand is weak.

Couple a lack of self-confidence with the level of stress we have in our daily lives, and the outlook can be even worse. The tragic part is that the impact of such manifestations can be terribly harsh on our personal brand perceptions. Interestingly enough, as with other gender distinctions, men and women exhibit stress very differently. As with anything else, there is an art to successful self-promotion. Self-promotion is *not* bragging. To know where to draw the line, all you need to keep in mind is the end result of your efforts. If you brag or boast too much, the end result is obvious—you will turn people off. So what makes self-promotion valid and acceptable? This is a common question. In fact, personal brand management is about self-promotion: owning your uniqueness and communicating it effectively to your target market.

Self-promotion is fine if it means you are explaining your uniqueness, raising awareness, and thereby explaining how you can help your target market. How else will you let people know what you do and how you can help them? You are all about helping the other person. Self-promotion is a healthy part of any successful business as well as a healthy part of the success of someone finding a job or getting promoted.

Self-glorification, or bragging, is when you no longer care about helping others but are looking to gain praise or attention.

If you have a strong personal branding strategy and self-promote with the intent of helping others, then you can never be rightfully accused of bragging or boasting, because you have a healthy and generous intent behind your self-promotion strategy.

So, consider what it would be like for you to know who you are, value your uniqueness and personal brand, share and promote yourself with self-confidence, and thus, attract business with ease and grace—all the while loving life and being happy. It is possible. It has happened, and continues to happen, to the women below. It can happen for you if you choose to allow yourself to develop your intentional personal brand.

Success Stories

The following success stories come from interviews with women lawyers who have successfully developed an intentional personal brand and used their personal brands to generate new business and enjoy a harmonious life. While there is no such thing as perfection or ultimate balance, these three women represent a comprehensive sampling of women balancing their personal and business lives well *and* being rainmakers. Their stories exemplify how to develop your own brand for rainmaking success. Let's look at how they have utilized their unique personal brands, successfully self-promoted with high self-confidence, and connected with their target markets while networking.

Pat Gillette
Partner, Orrick, Herrington & Sutcliffe
Employment Law

Pat Gillette has been developing her personal brand for success in her legal career for over 37 years as an employment law litigator. Pat is a wife, mother, and rainmaker, making time to serve her community and travel and speak. How does she do it so well?

We can measure Pat's success in any number of ways. For one thing, she has controlled annually between $3 and $10 million of business for over 25 years, which she attributes mainly to her personal brand, as she considers herself marketing daily with her personal brand.

When asked the key to her success, Pat says, "I started out just being myself—which includes being friendly, warm, [and] down to earth," among other things. "If you are being yourself, you will be successful. What won't work is trying to be someone or behave in a way that is not consistent with who you are."

Any effective personal brand starts with an understanding that you must be genuine and yourself. Otherwise, people sense the lack of the "real" you. So often we try to be an unnatural version of ourselves because we are trying to emulate others.

Owning who you are genuinely requires you to be self-confident and clear about your uniqueness. You don't need decades to gain clarity. You just need to be aware and put in the effort.

Pat cultivates self-confidence by "acknowleding that I am not great at all things. I have done a pretty good self-assessment, and I know that there are things I am as good at as anyone; there are other things that I am not so good at." As a result, Pat has a keen awareness of her uniqueness, what makes her special and confident, and owns it well within her personal brand.

There is nothing that shows our self-confidence as a personal brand more than acknowledging we cannot do everything well, nor do we want to. Plus, it helps to spread the work out so we are not always multitasking but showing up composed and in control.

Pat states, "I try to surround myself with people who complement my skill set. Then I can go into a meeting, or a trial, etcetera, with great confidence because I know I will do my part really well, and I count on others to carry out the additional aspects of the presentation. This doesn't mean that I don't stretch myself—but I don't try to be someone I am not."

In fact, Pat's advice to women includes a keen understanding that "women are hard on themselves and, as a result, may appear less confident. I want women to realize that we have many of the characteristics that make rainmakers successful: relationship building, charisma, listening skills, empathy, etcetera. So, I would encourage women to realistically identify their strengths, play to those strengths, and to not be afraid to talk about why they are good at what they do. I would also encourage women not to be afraid to take risks—put yourself out there and don't be discouraged if you fail the first or second time."

Often as women we find that networking is very difficult. We feel that we have to go to a networking event and do something extraordinary to "get business." Nothing is further from the truth. You just have to understand that any time you are out in public is a networking opportunity to be seen, to be heard, and to leave a strong first impression with your personal brand.

Attending networking events also means attending to learn from others and sharing something with them, thus giving and not just taking. This means, once again, being genuine and real and owning who you are. As Pat says, "I still am pretty much me in my interactions with clients, opposing counsel, and judges."

In personal brand management, in addition to knowing your uniqueness, you must know the story of "you" well so that you can share it genuinely when you are networking. Effectively communicating your personal brand will allow others to get to know you, the person, not just you, the lawyer. In that way, you leave a strong impression with high recall value for your audience. People with strong personal brands know their story well and are not afraid to share it, all the while balancing sharing with listening to the other party.

"When I write, when I talk, when I interact with people, I share information about myself. I may say that I am really happy because my kid got into graduate school or that I was elected to the city council in my town. By sharing personal stories about myself that highlight the strengths I have or showcase my interests, people get to know me pretty quickly. I often intertwine personal stories with discussions about business strategies to lighten the discussion and to encourage my clients to let me into their lives as well. The real secret is that I am very interested in other people and enjoy letting them get to know me personally so that I can get to know them. The same is true when I write or speak on issues. I don't try to be the ultimate legal voice on an issue—but I do want to be the practical voice, the creative voice, the strategic voice. So my writing and speaking is accessible, somewhat controversial, and always different from what everyone else is saying," notes Pat.

Karimah Lamar

Senior Associate, Carothers DiSante & Freudenberger LLP

Employment Law

It is not necessary to practice law for over 30 years, like Pat, to realize dividends as a rainmaker using your personal brand. Karimah Lamar, another employment litigator practicing for nine years, has been utilizing her intentional personal brand as a lawyer for marketing within the last year. Like Pat, Karimah is also a mother and wife and is active in her community, in addition to being a rainmaker and a woman lawyer.

"Prior to having a defined brand, I was not building quality relationships. I would attend different events, meet people, and rarely connect again. After I began to consciously think about my brand and develop it, my marketing efforts became more focused and purposeful.

I had a defined plan that allowed me to meet people, engage them, and actually create meaningful relationships," says Karimah.

Whenever we feel self-confident and communicate a strong brand, it is because we have passion and purpose for what we do as lawyers. This allows us to sell our services with a sense of ease and grace because people sense our passion and purpose.

Karimah cultivates self-confidence in this manner. "People typically lack self-confidence when they feel inferior to others. I love and enjoy what I do. There is no space for feeling inadequate when there is no doubt that as an experienced labor and employment attorney, I know that I am providing top-notch legal services to my clients."

Karimah utilizes the same strategy as Pat when networking, being interested rather than interesting. "[I] build relationships first, be of service second. So, when I meet people I am looking for a commonality, a way that we can connect. I really try and get to know people. The business relationship will flow naturally." Further, Karimah finds that being clear about her personal brand focuses her marketing efforts, thus allowing her to engage in activities that enhance and bring attention to her brand.

In addition, Karimah knows her uniqueness and shares her story well. She captures her target market's attention when networking or meeting with potential clients by making sure "they connect with my story, the collection of experiences that define who I am. Sharing that story is very intentional and allows me to cultivate relationships in a more intimate way. It is not just about selling my services, but building long-lasting relationships."

Karimah's advice for women lawyers aspiring to become rainmakers is simple: "Develop a personal brand. Be clear about what your brand is and consciously incorporate it into your marketing efforts."

Lori Lorenzo

Deputy Director, Leadership Council on Legal Diversity

Lori represents another facet of successful rainmaking as a female lawyer. Not only is Lori a successful lawyer, but she has developed her personal brand and rainmaking capabilities throughout her career, which has included owning a nonlegal franchise. She is featured because she is now second in command of a national nonprofit organization whose mission is to develop talented, diverse lawyers into leaders in the profession.

In fact, Lori attributes successfully attaining her job to her personal brand. "Having a strong brand launched me into a position with a national spotlight. The competition was stiff, and to assume the role, I needed not only a solid brand, but a group of sponsors that already knew my brand well and were willing to help me market it. Without those 'loyal consumers,' I wouldn't be where I am today."

Lori is the single mother of four children, three of whom have special needs. She is an excellent example of a woman lawyer who knows who she is as a personal brand, understands her story, and communicates it well to attract business and buzz.

Lori has developed a keen awareness of why personal branding matters. "I first realized that I had a brand and that I had to intentionally develop my brand about five years ago. When I was a small business owner, I realized that to compete for discretionary income dollars, I needed to differentiate my service from what my competitors provided. My brand then began and ended with the highest level of personalized customer service. When I returned to the world of law practice after owning my business, I realized that my brand would be important because there is tremendous competition. In other words, the personal relationships I had relied upon when I owned a small business couldn't be my only tactic; I needed to build personal relationships, and then ask those people to spread my brand to their networks. That realization prompted me to refine and articulate my brand and my value proposition."

Lori balances her life well. In fact, it is how she cultivates self-confidence. "I have noticed over time that I am most self-confident when I remember to engage myself in the things that matter most to me. For me, those things include exercise, healthy eating, and quality time with close friends and family. When these things aren't included in my life, my self-confidence wanes. I want to be sure to note that the balance is difficult to maintain. Early in my career, it was nearly impossible because I hadn't identified the components of a personal brand. Later in my career, it synced, and then I got divorced. As a single mom to four kids, three of whom have special needs or are classified as children with special needs, the balance virtually disappeared. Finding my rhythm again was challenging; there was so much judgment: 'You travel that much and still want to leave your kids on Saturday morning to go to the gym' or 'You're not coming to the parent-teacher conference . . . again.' Work colleagues have questioned both my loyalty to work and my maternal instincts. Ultimately, I remind myself that I have the best interests of my kids at heart and I'm doing the best I can to create the best life for them. Luckily, my kids provide plenty of affirmation that our family is OK. I think that now, I know the

> *"I have to remain true to my brand and only change when I've thoughtfully considered the implications."*

best way to cultivate self-confidence is to pay attention to how I feel and how those that are close to me are feeling," says Lori.

For Lori, knowing her uniqueness has helped her hone her story and use it well with others. She has spent time discovering her uniqueness and owns it very genuinely. Moreover, she has learned when and how to selectively and impactfully share her story for maximum connection and effect. As Lori points out, at first she overshared her story in an attempt to connect, and risked alienating people. Then, she withdrew and didn't share herself. Now, she has taken time, patience, and reinvention to refine her approach to sharing her personal brand.

"I've spent a great deal of time thinking about what the three most important features of my brand are and how those parts resonate with different audiences. The three most important pieces of my brand are that I am great on stage and knowledgeable in front of audiences; I travel, which helps me identify as a person that builds relationships in person; and, that I'm a single mom. The last of those is really the one I try to use as my go-to, which may seem counterintuitive. But, I believe that if the first two are done well, they speak for themselves, and then the onus is on me to share my personal story. I believe that if people know that I'm a single mom to four kids and they connect that with the speaking and the travel, I can start to break down stereotypes about working moms and what it means to be a good mom. In addition, I want to encourage the generation of women coming after me to know that work and family can be done. It's very important, however, to know your audience. For example, I didn't march into my first board of directors meeting with my mom badge shining brightly. I developed relationships and shared my mom stories selectively, then let my work product settle in, and finally began sharing my personal story more broadly. When I speak to law students, I let the family part of my story lead. Sometimes, I think my personal story helps others to understand my professional story; sometimes my professional story has to come first, before someone is ready to hear my personal story," says Lori.

Like the other rainmakers with strong personal brands, Lori has experienced her frustrations. Most notably, she has been successful because she keeps in mind that only a genuine and honest personal brand sells and attracts business. "The most frustrating part is remaining true to my brand. I've learned that I will always be faced with opportunities to dilute my brand, or change my brand to fit the needs of a person or organization, but if I want to stay happily employed, I have to remain true to my brand and only change when I've thoughtfully considered the implications."

Another trait that these women and all successful women rainmakers utilizing their personal brands well have realized is that the content of your personal brand is an ongoing, evolutionary process. You must always be aware of your brand and refine it as you grow and change in any stage of your personal life and legal career. You cannot develop a personal brand and forget about it. You must continue tweaking it over time. Stale personal brands fail.

Conclusion

In summary, the first step to being a successful woman rainmaker requires you to intentionally create a personal brand. This personal brand must be a genuine reflection of who you are as a *person*, not as a lawyer. As we have seen with our women rainmaker examples, your personal brand must utilize your uniqueness and your story. You must convey it with self-confidence, knowing you are worth the self-promotion and the connection value with others. All of this takes time, patience, and revision. Do not assume that your personal brand is secondary to your substantive career. Owning your personal brand is necessary to highlight your legal career and attract business.

When you have an intentional personal brand, you will find your stress is lower and your self-confidence is higher. People will sense this in you and will be interested to get to know you. They will presume correctly that you must be an excellent lawyer and worth being hired.

Here's to your personal brand. It takes courage and self-awareness to develop it and time to own it.

Chapter 8

Making the Pitch

Jeana Goosmann

The perfect pitch isn't just for baseball. Making the perfect pitch can bring in new clients, create long-lasting personal connections, and boost your chances of future business opportunities. Start making proposals to clients and prospects early in your career to help build your reputation and get noticed. Growing a book of business can be fun and exhilarating and make you a rainmaker.

Rainmakers land clients. Rainmakers leverage their vast connections and personal relationships and turn contacts into paying streams of revenue. They start by understanding and anticipating the needs of the client. They don't just tell prospects rehearsed rhetoric; they show potential clients that they care about their business and about solving their problem. They've done their homework and know the right questions to ask in the meeting so they are prepared to jump when an opportunity arises. This may mean reading a client's book to better understand their needs or researching every public resource to get to know the client. Research and being prepared are crucial in the initial meeting phase.

Rainmakers are different. They stand out from the pack. Sometimes it's the little things that can make a big difference. You don't always need a grand entrance and polished boardroom to stand out. Going back to the basics of being polite and listening to what the other person has to say can be just as influential. Maybe you do something creative such as giving your potential client who adores his or her furry friend a gourmet dog biscuit wrapped up with Fido's name on the tag. Be gracious and remember *please* and *thank you*.

Throughout this chapter, you will read the interviews of four women rainmakers who have found ways to engage new business from making the pitch. From personal connections to research and ways to stand out, these women share their experiences of what works and how you can integrate their best practices in your career.

Jennifer P. Bagg

Partner, Wiltshire & Grannis LLP

Communications Law and Policy

Jennifer first began giving presentations to prospects straight out of law school as a junior associate working in a small boutique practice. As she grew her business, she saw the advantages of continuing to meet with potential clients. By the time she was a midlevel associate, she was engaging in her own client development activities, such as attending networking events, setting up meetings with prospects, and launching new work. Jennifer has been practicing for ten years and is a partner at Wiltshire & Grannis LLP, a small firm of 30 lawyers. The firm focuses in communications law and litigation, while Jennifer primarily focuses her practice on communications law and policy. Jennifer spends approximately 10 percent of her time marketing and promoting herself and is someone who gets in front of potential clients, and ultimately receives new business from it.

Jennifer says, "Having my own book of business gave me the flexibility to move to a new law firm when I determined that would be the best decision for my career. Moreover, I have a seat at the table when it comes to firm strategy and decision making. Given my success in pitching new work, the firm also calls on me to participate when client development opportunities arise."

Taking an informal approach to giving a proposal was how Jennifer initially started to grow her practice. "I benefit from working in a practice area that has an extraordinary association that makes it easy to network. The Federal Communications Bar Association [FCBA] puts on brown bag lunches and CLEs for subspecialty areas, sponsors formal lunches with industry leaders as speakers, and hosts other activities, such as an annual seminar and volunteer opportunities. FCBA members include attorneys that work in private practice, for the government, in-house, at associations, and for nonprofits. Participation in the FCBA was invaluable to getting to know prospects. Through interactions related to my practice area, I was able to approach potential clients informally about work opportunities. Through speaking on panels and participating in brown bag–style lunch discussions, I was able to raise my profile to potential clients.

In recent years, I have set up more formal pitches, but these typically have only arisen from networking and more informal opportunities," says Jennifer.

After raising her profile, Jennifer began to see new business begin pouring in. "My first new business came from making a pitch to an existing client of the firm when I was around a seven-year associate. It was a significant, long-term project that I was asked to manage and take the lead on. My first time bringing a new client to the firm was as a senior associate (around eight years), and within a matter of months, I had brought in several new clients."

> *"My first time bringing a new client to the firm was as a senior associate. . ., and within a matter of months, I had brought in several new clients."*

Jennifer understood that gaining new business from a proposal doesn't happen overnight, but she saw the benefits from it and then in turn reaped the rewards. "The more I interacted with existing and potential clients, the more comfortable I became with asking the clients for meetings to discuss work opportunities," she explains. "These meetings were rarely very formal. Rather, they were an opportunity to discuss the needs the client had and how the firm could potentially help. I was able to gauge the success of these meetings by the client calling or emailing me directly with assignments."

Jennifer worked in-house internationally early in her career. During that time, she sent out a formal request for proposal (RFP) to ten law firms that she knew by reputation to help the company with a specific project. Ultimately, the company chose counsel based on other factors beyond the RFP response. Now that Jennifer is in private practice, if she receives an RFP, her decision to respond or not depends on who the client is.

If Jennifer does do a formal pitch, she researches the company through public Securities and Exchange Commission (SEC) filings and puts together a great team with herself and a big-name partner, plus someone else who will actually do the work. Rather than prepare elaborate presentations in the formal pitch, she finds that the potential client "just wants to talk to us." In order to make it flow, she does an overview of the firm and their expertise. Then she gets into the particulars of the project and assigns roles to the presenters so it can be a dialogue with the client. Jennifer can usually tell by the end of the conversation if the firm is going to meet the client's needs, but regardless, she always follows up in the next few days to say thank you for the opportunity. The best pitches end with the client awarding the work on the spot and Jennifer walking out feeling great with a signed engagement agreement.

Jennifer noticed the need to be patient as she was looking to expand her business and receive new clients. "This certainly did not and does not always work, if the firm does not immediately receive work from the potential client, but I still think the process is beneficial. In my specialized area of practice, there is an ebb and flow of work that clients need and the lawyers they turn to [to] do the work. By setting up the informal meetings to discuss work opportunities, I am ensuring that the potential client will keep me in mind as they have future legal needs that arise."

Jennifer is experienced in informal presentations and the initial meeting, but she can still recall some frustrations she has had along the way. "My greatest frustration was when I did not see immediate results and when the potential clients I had been networking with would contact the partners at the firm instead of contacting me directly. The partners I worked for reminded me I was still quite junior in the eyes of the clients, and, fortunately, the partners for the most part recognized my contribution to the client development process."

Jennifer's advice to other women lawyers is to be proactive and know your client and their industry. She finds that young lawyers skip getting to know how the client's business actually works and learning the technology, while she has made her entire career around it. Jennifer frequently will ask the client to send over their engineers to explain the technology to her in her office, where they draw diagrams on the whiteboard together so that she can know the facts and can speak the language before she applies the law and makes a legal proposal. She'll take pictures of the whiteboard before it is erased to keep in her file. "Growing your book of business may take some time; however, being proactive about the end goal will benefit you more than doing nothing at all."

Amy Conners
Partner, Best & Flanagan LLP
Complex Commercial Litigation

Amy Conners has been practicing for 11 years and is a partner at Best & Flanagan in Minneapolis, Minnesota. Amy was introduced to pitching proposals early on in her career through taking part in researching and presenting to potential clients as an assignment. Being included in delivering a proposal, she learned from her mentors the significance of knowing as much about the client as possible and trying to see the problem from their perspective. She has grown to understand the importance of doing your homework prior to the meeting and anticipating the client's needs. A guiding principal in her preparation is "View the problem from the client's point of view and make it personal."

"When I was a first-year attorney, I was at a firm in New York where we were expected to develop our marketing skills," Amy recalls. "I remember early on working on background research and other attorneys making the pitch. I went along with partners as a junior attorney and in some cases because I had a particular school connection." Amy later moved back to Minnesota, where she continued to hone her pitch skills. "I went on a pitch where I had worked with the potential client as a general counsel. Even though I didn't have the experience of the senior attorneys, I was still able to make that personal connection."

Amy capitalized on her problem solving for one client as a way to pitch to other potential clients. She had advised a client who was having issues with text messages, which is an evolving area of law. Then, based on her research and helping that client deal with the issue, she was able to advise other clients on how to get their compliance programs in line and proactively give another client advice to generate new business for herself.

Research and building personal connections has helped Amy set up meetings with potential clients. Although her presentations and delivery of proposals have evolved, the way she sets up her deliveries has not changed. "I set them up in person. I've also written articles that I've shared via email or LinkedIn; that would be for reaching a broader audience," Amy explains. "I think people really value that personal connection. You can meet them over lunch or coffee; it doesn't have to be a formal meeting."

Whether meeting with a potential client for the first time or the fifth time, Amy always begins with research. "I like to be as prepared as possible for pitches: working on research, learning the law and as much about the client ahead of time. Also, learning as much about the problem ahead of time and how they feel about it. Then, you can target your pitch to show you're on the same page as them and want to achieve the solutions that they are thinking of."

In order to achieve a solution, you have to understand the problem. Discussing the problem during the presentation and the ways you can achieve a solution will be a key part to winning over a potential client. Amy elaborates: "I talked to the main contacts I had at a company and was asked to be one of a couple of law firms that were making a pitch for work. I asked my contact, What do you want to see done? What is your most favorable outcome here? What is the problem you are facing? How is it affecting you? How is it affecting your vendors? and How is it affecting your stakeholders? Once I had that information, I used it to target my legal research and ultimately draft a presentation that would address the needs that they had."

Once she understands the problem, Amy is able to draft a presentation and structure it so it won't overwhelm the client. "It evolved. It started with an outline in a detailed memo of where I wanted to go. I like to get into the details, so I did research too. Then, I took that and put it into a PowerPoint so we can have the details there without overwhelming the client."

Amy will spend anywhere between 15 to 20 hours, plus the hours of a junior associate, drafting a presentation. She has experienced the value in that preparation firsthand. Amy says, "I think potential clients definitely find that to be of added value. It is something they like to see because I am giving them my services for free and have already thought about it and mapped out the strategy. In some pitches, I've gone into drafting and mapping it out to show them this is what I'd do and this is where I'd go. Getting their feedback right at the meeting is helpful if they can see that you were putting thought into it." Amy also mentioned that clients are often surprised when she has drafted documents at the initial

> *"I think that the more you can get to know people on a personal level, the better it's going to go."*

meeting phase. "I think they are surprised. I don't do it all the time. But, I think it's really helpful and shows that you're dedicated to solving their problems by getting their input at an early stage."

Having a pleasantly surprised client in the initial meeting phase is an excellent way to get them and eventually gain their work long-term. When Amy wants to get on-board this stage, she assembles a proposal team with various experiences. Amy says, "You want to get the team that has the best depth of experience so you can show the clients that this is going to be a big deal. You are going to have the people that will anticipate their needs with a variety of experience levels, and the background to help with that." Amy will often bring in an outside expert to go along on the pitch. "We will talk about who we will have, and these are the types of experts we want to engage," Amy explains. "I've used former FBI agents a lot in interviews to prep clients and get their buy-in early on."

Amy will prep her team ahead of time to make sure the proposal is seamless and everyone involved is as prepared as possible. "It comes together pretty easily; once you know what the problem is, you can get the right team of people. You want someone that has the experience and stature and gravitas that they are going to need, especially if it's a really expensive matter. They want to know someone like that is working on the case and knowing that there are also people in the trenches that are very good. I think it is good to introduce all those people, if not in person, than at least tell them in the meeting who you envision being on the team," explains Amy. "Diversity is also really important to a lot of clients. That is a factor we take into account. Looking to have a diverse team is always ideal."

Along with a diverse team, Amy finds it important to add a personal touch to every pitch. "I think that the more you can get to know people on a personal level, the better it's going to go. That's why it's important if you have somebody that has a personal relationship, you definitely want them at the pitch to make it less businesslike and more friendly. Also, you want potential clients to have that feeling that they can call you at any time, that you have their back. Trying to convey that you are available is important. Giving cell phone information, being able to connect with the people, and also getting their questions heard," says Amy. Personalizing the pitch may seem difficult if you don't know the client on that level; however, Amy believes that doing your homework beforehand to understand the potential client and their interests will pay off in the end.

Amy and her team use smart creativity to make their pitch stand out. "I think it goes to doing the due diligence ahead of time. Don't just rely on the website, but do a lot of research on who you're meeting with. For example, a client we were meeting with wrote a book. We tried to have as many people on the team read the book ahead of time and really get to know what he was thinking. Get to know the potential client as much as possible, and then show that you have that level of knowledge. It shows that you're dedicated," says Amy.

To structure her proposal, Amy uses an approach that first addresses the issue, shows a preview of what their recommendations will be, and includes an overview of the legal analysis, a timeline, and opportunities for negotiation. Amy explains, "Help them create a road map to get to the outcome. It's a conversation that takes place where you're getting a lot of information, but also seeking input along the way. Then, close with a preview of the budget and explain this is how we think we can do it. Talk about any alternative fee arrangements (if that is a possibility), thank them for their time, and ask for the work."

In order to anticipate the needs of a potential client, it is important that everyone is on the same page, one of those being the budget. Addressing a budget in the first initial meeting with a potential client may seem awkward or uncomfortable. However, Amy shared her advice to put yourself at ease when addressing a budget. She says, "I think being as straightforward as possible and showing that you're open to alternative fee arrangements is important. Finding out from them what their budgetary needs are, what time of the year those fees might hit, and showing you are able to work with them on that. Budget communication is best done up front."

Heidi McNeil Staudenmaier
Partner, Snell & Wilmer
Federal Indian Law and Gaming Law

Heidi McNeil Staudenmaier has been practicing for almost 30 years in federal Indian law and gaming law and is a senior partner at Snell & Wilmer, a large firm with multiple offices in the Southwest region of the United States. She first started practicing law as a trial lawyer, but also had an interest in federal Indian law based upon a law school class at the University of Iowa College of Law. When the Federal

Indian Gaming Regulatory Act was passed by Congress in 1988, she recognized the great opportunity and potential in the Indian gaming industry. Little did she know that tribal gaming would grow into a nearly $30 billion industry by 2012.

She first became involved in presenting proposals by spending much of her own time learning and researching her area of law. And, like Jennifer Bagg, Heidi also used networking and speaking engagements to help grow her book of business. Heidi says, "Initially, I had one client interested in exploring opportunities in tribal gaming. Recognizing the potential, I spent considerable time on my own learning the ins and outs of the Federal Indian Gaming Regulatory Act, which included attending any available seminars. I also started looking for avenues where I could have articles published, speaking opportunities, etcetera. Slowly but surely, I developed national recognition on tribal gaming issues. Based on that national recognition, I started receiving more and more inquiries from potential clients, which ultimately led to more and more business."

Heidi makes sure that she is constantly delivering presentations to keep the work flow fresh to lead to more business. "I don't think anyone should ever be satisfied with their current client base—I think they constantly need to be looking for new opportunities. Particularly in the area of law that I'm doing, there's been a lot of consolidation lately. Someday, one of my current clients may get acquired by somebody else and that other entity may be using other counsel and may not require me to stay involved."

Delivering proposals and meeting with potential clients is something that must be constantly kept up on, and Heidi has found that she gets many formal RFPs within her niche. "We get quite a few RFPs, particularly from Indian tribes and tribal entities looking for different types of counsel with different needs," says Heidi.

Requests for proposals help promote healthy competition among businesses within that industry. A business in need of a specific service, skill, or product will send an RFP to a few firms.

"Lately, it seems that they aren't asking for in-person meetings. Sometimes they want to do it by conference call or do it based on the submitted proposal. It all depends on the RFP and their legal need. If they are looking for labor and employment expertise or corporate expertise, which isn't really my area, I will take along somebody who would be an expert in that area." Heidi will choose her presenting team that goes with her for the formal delivery or conference call based on the potential client's needs. "You don't want to have too many people attending. It's kind of a balancing act of showing them you are interested and that you have a capable team with several people going, as opposed to taking a team of ten."

With conference calling becoming more popular than in-person meetings, Heidi has also done some video conferencing to deliver her proposal. Giving a proposal over the phone is very different than doing so in an in-person meeting. Just as Amy Conners does her research to be prepared for a meeting, Heidi makes sure that both she and the potential client are properly prepped for the meeting. Heidi will make sure that the other individual has all the necessary materials in hand during the call. "First I want to make sure they have my materials, at least in front of them visually, by either email or hard copy. I try not to just go over the materials, but to give the highlights and keep it short. I want to make sure that I know what their specific questions are, so I try to make an initial introduction and overview, and then refer them to the highlights of our response. Then I open it up to questions to find out what they really are interested in," says Heidi.

Heidi delivers both cold-call presentations as well as formal RFPs. "Cold call," she explains, "is a combination of referrals or somebody I know who told me about this opportunity and they wanted to see if I was interested. Then, if I say yes, they go ahead and send it to me. Some of these come from different contacts I have, so it really varies."

Differentiating yourself from the pack of other law firms and attorneys trying to win over the same client can be a challenge, but Heidi brings it back to the basics by suggesting that you tell the potential client what makes you and your firm unique. "I highlight that there is only a handful of attorneys out there that do what I do and have been doing it for as long as I've done it. I try to make sure they are aware of my expertise and the wide range of experience that I have. I also try to highlight that we are a large law firm and that we have resources in all of our offices that we can bring to the relationship. We can provide them with one-stop shopping for the engagement as opposed to having to seek out counsel in specific areas."

> *"I think it's very important, even if you don't win the deal, that you find out as much as you can about why they didn't pick you,"*

To close a proposed offer in an RFP, Heidi finds the follow-up process crucial. She explains, "I think you always need to stay in touch once you deliver the information to them and you actually do the pitch; you can't just sit back. You don't want to be a pest about bothering them, but you want to find out what the timing is for the decision-making process. You need to be informed about how they are going to make their decision and then based on that, you figure out what kind of follow-up you should do. I usually like to follow up by thanking them for the time and [asking] if there is any additional information we can provide. Then, if you don't hear back from them in a week, you need to follow up tactfully to see if they have made a decision."

Heidi believes that you should ask why they did or didn't hire you. She has found that there is an incredible amount of information that can be brought out in asking that question that will help as you develop proposals in the future. "I think it's very important, even if you don't win the deal, that you find out as much as you can about why they didn't pick you," says Heidi. Along with asking the right questions during the close, timing is also very important.

"If I am aware of a key decision that came down or an important policy, I have an immediate email list—and send it to that email list. It's essential to be timely because if it's going to impact a potential client, they appreciate, first, being told about it, and second, being able to call you. Keep yourself current on your area of expertise so that people know you are on top of things at all times," says Heidi.

Heidi's advice to younger lawyers is to build good client relationships. Heidi explains, "A lot of times they may be dealing with younger lawyers in-house, maybe not the general counsel, but maybe one of the staff attorneys. Those staff attorneys may become general counsel, and they're going to remember the younger people in the firm they are working with, as opposed to a senior partner. I think it is very important for younger attorneys to do the best work they can. When they have a client relationship, they need to be responsive, timely, and build the best relationship possible."

With about 30 years of experience practicing law, Heidi has encountered some frustrations along the way when developing a presentation, but with experience also comes patience. Like Jennifer Bagg, Heidi noticed that it takes time to begin developing business after a pitch. Heidi says, "The most frustrating part, initially, was just being patient. You can't expect business to immediately drop in your lap overnight. You need to spend a lot of personal time, nonbillable, developing your expertise and then figuring out how best to market it. You need to constantly make the pitch and market yourself—ultimately, you will succeed. Don't give up! My motto: 'Be a shameless self-promoter.'"

Paula Pace

Partner, Bryan Cave LLP

Business Finance, Treasury, and Derivative Products

Paula Pace is a partner at Bryan Cave LLP, a large multinational firm, and has been practicing since 1984. Her areas of practice are business finance, treasury, and derivative products. Paula has discovered that the theme of respect and being polite has not only made her presentations successful, but has made her clients appreciate her legal advice and continue giving her work.

Paula began delivering presentations in a "purposeful manner" in 2004 while participating in a program developed within her firm that focuses on the successful practices of known rainmakers. Her first step was to abandon efforts to fit into a preconceived mold of what she thought was expected of her to "behave like a lawyer." Her strategy to get more pitches became an overall change in how she lived her life, which primarily included focusing on behaving authentically, listening intently to her clients and potential clients. That included digging for the "real" or underlying issue that was important to clients and prospects. Paula decided to stand out in more ways than one to differentiate herself. She says, "At a cocktail party attended by potential clients and lawyers all wearing similar blue suits, I have learned that to be memorable and viewed as different from the rest, the best strategy is to present one's authentic personality and listen intently to what prospects have to say." Paula also explains, "We all tend to let our minds wander during conversations, or to think we already know the answer to someone's needs within a few sentences. What the potential client really wants is to be heard."

Paula used listening to her clients' needs to help grow relationships and her reputation, which are large factors in becoming skilled in your craft and can take time to gradually build. "I think most of us get business by having very good relationships with our clients. That started for me as a young attorney working with other clients at Bryan Cave and having them refer me to others. There comes a point where making the pitch comes into play. I think that there are a lot of people that rely on doing very good work and having that meaningful relationship with the client. Yet there's a way to say 'I'd like to get more business from you.' Or asking the client, 'We have a great relationship, you know me, you know my skills, and yet I don't seem to be getting a lot of work from you; what can I do to get that work?" says Paula. With time, Paula has learned how to become comfortable asking for more business. Once Paula is sufficiently comfortable with her client and she does not think it would be awkward to ask, she will. "As I've gotten older, I have more experience and confidence in my own skills and my own ability and providing work where my client believes that I have their best interests at heart. I'm less afraid to ask that question than I used to be, but I think you have to be up front about it. If you come across in any manner false or insincere, then it will sour even the best relationship."

Paula believes that good relationships and confidence will help gain more business and land more pitches. What's the worst thing someone can do? Paula says, "Trying to pretend like they want to have a deep relationship with the person they are just meeting or pretending like they can't wait to get to know them when really the point of the meeting is to present the firm and what we can do for them. I think that the best thing you can do is be up front, and say, 'I'd like to meet you for lunch and tell you more about Bryan Cave.'"

Afraid to ask for business in a meeting? Paula has experienced that most often attorneys get business from the one-on-one relationship with their current clients. She has discovered that most clients don't know you want more business. Her advice is to be honest and not afraid to ask for their business.

After getting past the fear of asking for business, Paula has found that preparation and how your team members coordinate with one another while working together are key factors in a successful presentation. "My best success story is where a group of us went to respond to an RFP. I think we were scheduled for maybe an hour, and we ended up having such a wonderful time it went well beyond that hour. Ultimately, we got all the work. The client said when we were in the pitch, they could tell that we were all straightforward folks who liked one another and obviously supported one another. I think it depends on the structure of the firm in terms of how people are rewarded for work, but we have a system within our firm that rewards everyone for their role and we feel it promotes the sharing of credit. Because of that, I think we are happy to go help and support one another, and that ease of being with one another and that promotion of each other shows." Sincerity and being yourself go a long way, according to Paula.

Asking questions and listening deeply to what the client says may seem like a simple task, but for some it is an unlearned trait or one that we need to be reminded of every now and then. "I think in many respects, a lot of us have lost the ability to be polite," Paula observes.

Paula has numerous ways that she makes her proposals creative and personalized. "When we have a client that we know has a dog, we will bring dog biscuits. That's another way to actually form a deep relationship with a client—know their interests. To the extent that you know somebody's interest and then you bring something that is a nod to that interest is very effective, and it shows that you worked hard enough to find out what they care about and what they like. You are showing them respect for what it is that they like," says Paula.

Showing respect by finding what the client cares about helps you earn the client's trust, lightens the mood, and puts the potential client at ease. Paula also suggests sharing a funny story about yourself during the presentation or initial meeting. Paula says, "I can rarely talk to anybody without telling them a funny story about myself. I am a pretty informal person, so when I work with clients or meet clients I tend to let that be known. I'm not a naturally funny person, but things that happen to me in my life tend to make people laugh. That puts people at ease, because it makes them generally relax around you."

In the closing of every pitch, Paula gives advice about how you can make the deal happen during the closing of every pitch. "At the end, just like any good oral argument, summarize what you just said. Make sure that there are no questions that go unanswered, or if there is anything else, ask the question, 'Is there any additional information that you need from us?' You write it down and you make sure you respond to it. Once you leave you always, *always*, thank them for their time. I always send a note to them including something that they revealed during the course of the conversation, and comment on that when I thank them. It shows that you listened and it shows you cared about what they said. Again, it's a matter of showing respect to that person and who they are and the time they spent with you."

Conclusion

After hearing the experiences and shared stories of Jennifer, Amy, Heidi, and Paula, you've learned the benefits of delivering a proposal and the importance of personal connections and doing your homework. You've found ways to handle RFPs, and have heard that being polite and authentic can bring you business. Now is the time to get started and put a plan into action.

Chapter 9

Technology and the Law

Traci Ray, with Interviews by Mavis Gragg

Welcome to the technology chapter! This chapter is all about software and mobile applications that can improve law practice efficiency—results-oriented tools you can use to enhance and grow your business. From basic software and apps, to managing relationships with current and prospective clients, to more sophisticated programs tailored to give you strong ROI, the pages that ensue will equip you with the knowledge and tools to build a tech strategy to generate business that caters to your needs, resources, and abilities. My goal is to help you become familiar with the unknown and figure out how your practice can best benefit from all the offerings out there, with a focus on efficiency and results that lead to more business. In this chapter, I will introduce you to five female lawyers who successfully use technology as a rainmaking tool. Through their interviews, we will discover how virtual law offices, live chat windows, marketing videos, telephone technologies, customized software, and smart phone apps are significantly enhancing the way they are developing and managing business.

Rachel Rodgers

Founding Partner, Rachel Rodgers
Law Office

Intellectual Property Strategy

Rachel Rodgers of Rachel Rodgers Law Office practices in New York and New Jersey, where she focuses on IP strategy and works with digital entrepreneurs and small business owners to anticipate and protect the legal needs of

159

their business. Rachel has found much success running her practice as a virtual law office (VLO). VLO is the term used for legal practices that do not utilize traditional office space, but rather capitalize on technology to successfully practice law. Therefore, a VLO is a platform that allows the lawyer to offer services to clients by capitalizing on online tools. There are many variations of virtual offices that include lawyers working from home full time, lawyers subletting office space or conference rooms for just a few days a month (usually when meeting with clients), or lawyers contracting with a VLO company that provides a package deal including mail service (so an attorney can have her mail sent to a public location and not her home or a PO box), receptionist/messaging, and professional office space available on an "as-needed" basis.

Many attorneys who choose to run a virtual law office are solo practitioners. The costs associated with running one's own firm can be staggering. VLOs offer a major cost-saving option. With a tough market over the past few years, more and more new lawyers have opened up their own shops, and many have found great success with the VLO model—keeping costs in check while maintaining a professional appearance and meeting ethical requirements.

Rachel explains that her VLO gives her exceptional value and offers her clients easier access to her services. Most of her client meetings are done over Skype or through her online portal. She uses MyCase, which is integrated with her website, to send clients messages via email. Her clients then log in to the online portal, receive messages, review their documents, and even pay their bills. A major benefit, according to Rachel, is that "I don't have clients' emails in my inbox. I don't have the security issue with [them] being in my inbox, and [this] allows for better management of emails and time."

Rachel also uses Infusionsoft, a client relationship management software. Infusionsoft boasts many tools, including CRM (customer relationship management), which centralizes all customer interactions and daily activities in one place. Infusionsoft also offers email marketing and lead scoring, which is a method used to rank prospects. One major ranking factor is the interaction with the potential client— such as when the client opens an email, downloads an attachment, or clicks to your website. Rachel loves being able to track all the links on her website to see what people are clicking on and how they come to her website. Rachel emphasizes that once she gets all of the tracking information, the follow-up is the most important piece of the puzzle. She actually created her own Infusionsoft form that she fills out when talking to a potential client. The completed form then goes to her assistant, who sends the potential client a follow-up email. Rachel has created and automated the follow-up process to fully utilize each and every opportunity to sign a new client. Despite all the technology involved, Rachel is able to maintain a personal touch, and that type of follow-up sets her VLO apart from the competition.

Furthermore, all of Rachel's emails go through FuseDesk, an Infusionsoft application. Emails coming though FuseDesk are all assigned to the party responsible for addressing them. Rachel has multiple templates that her office uses to respond to the emails. The beauty of it is that when someone sends her an email, FuseDesk will add it to the contact's profile in Infusionsoft. If she later receives a call from Mike Jones, she can pull him up and see all of their past interactions—meaning she does not need to worry about keeping countless interactions and details top of mind. She worked with someone for six months to set up this program, but now she confirms that it saves her a significant amount of time and energy on a daily basis. Once FuseDesk was systemized, she felt like she was working a little less and making a little more.

Rachel's advice when it comes to VLOs and incorporating technology into the practice of law: "If you can get through law school, you can figure out how to use software." So there you have it—you have the abilities; you just have to take that leap from "how it's always been done" to "how you're going to take your practice to the next level."

Another way Rachel is using technology to differentiate her firm and impact her bottom line is through the use of marketing videos on her website. These are usually short videos that act as teasers by briefly explaining the firm's expertise or answering "the top things you should know or consider about X." Marketing videos may even take the form of client testimonials that can shine a very positive third-party light on the firm in a way that is relatable to potential clients. The advantages of marketing videos are many, including enhancing search engine optimization (SEO) for your website, providing meaningful content for potential clients, and serving to demonstrate your firm's personality and command of the areas in which the firm practices.

Rachel uses video to market her practice and explains that the content she offers for free usually "shows people that they need a lawyer." The idea of giving consumers just enough information to realize that they don't know enough is an important component of marketing videos. Showcasing that you are the go-to for their issues, and that you have the answers, is the next step, and a staple of this technology.

When videos are done well, they are a great tool. If you plan to use marketing videos, thoughtfully consider having the videos professionally produced. Just because we can all film a short clip with our phones does not mean we should do so, even though the cost is low and therefore enticing. Invest in the videos as you would with any other piece of your marketing—no shortcuts allowed. Also, it is advisable that you avoid setting the movie clips to auto-start, blasting onto the screen and through the speakers. Instead, consider using a "Click Here to Play" or a "Question & Answer" format to welcome the interested party and engage him or her willingly. Just like ensuring we size the pop-up video chat window correctly to fit mobile devices, we want the marketing video technology to work in our favor, not against us by turning potential clients into irritated consumers who click on that red "X" in the corner, passing us by. And last but not least, it is a good idea to consider posting your high-quality videos to YouTube as well—there is a double benefit for the same cost. By making your movie searchable on YouTube, you can drive more traffic to your site, be on a huge platform in addition to your own site, and—perhaps the best part—pay nothing to have your video working double time for you.

Nicole S. Biddle

Partner, Burton Law LLC

Transactions and Compliance

Nicole S. Biddle, with Burton Law LLC, handles corporate law, commercial litigation; creditors' rights and bankruptcy; and administrative, regulatory, and compliance matters. Nicole practices in Kentucky and the District of Columbia. She is a huge proponent of the VLO model, stating that "the mobility and flexibility to meet the needs of clients, especially in a changing legal environment, are of the utmost importance. Any working mother like me appreciates the ability to spend more time with family and with marketing." She also reinforces the money-saving aspect of a VLO because the overhead is much less. When Nicole needs an office, she simply uses Davinci Office Space, which has a network of offices available around the country. Additionally, Nicole has been able to take the savings the firm gets from working as a VLO and using tech applications and pass those savings on to the clients. In other words, to Nicole, a VLO equates to lower rates for her clients, and charging lower rates equates to a very marketable piece of her practice. The bottom line is that lower rates make Nicole even more competitive in the legal marketplace.

The VLO model also frees up a lot of time and money to use for client development. Everything is streamlined through technology. Burton Law employs multiple technologies in the VLO practice, and some of Nicole's favorites include the following:

1. Curo Legal: An outsourcing tool for day-to-day activities (billing, bookkeeping, filing services, paralegal services). Curo also provides notarization services, which lessens Nicole's need to meet face-to-face with her clients to execute documents. It supports her practice because it saves on overhead and time.

2. Box.com and Dropbox: Nicole's firm recently began exploring a paperless practice. This includes using electronic signatures as well as programs such as Box.com, an application her firm uses to hold the documents in a place where any attorney has access to them no matter her location or ability to connect with the firm's server, and Dropbox, a file maintenance system where emails are sent out to the users to keep everyone up to date if and when changes to the documents are made.

3. Clio: This program is built with the notion of saving time when it comes to client and matter management, QuickBooks, calendars and reminders, timesheets and activity tracking, time reports, online bill paying, and more. Nicole's office finds Clio's time-keeping, note-taking, file-tracking, and communications tools to be extremely helpful.

4. Google Hangouts and Skype: Like many VLO users, Nicole has found that meeting with clients virtually, if there is a need to meet face-to-face, is extremely easy and absolutely a cost saver. Travel time and related expenses are completely non-existent, and one doesn't even need an office to meet in.

Nicole admits that "there is definitely a learning curve. I have had to make sure that I ask questions and that I really understand how the technology works so I can use it correctly." However, as Rachel affirms above, Nicole agrees that "once you understand the technology, you really find that it helps your practice." To be very specific, Nicole pointed to benefits such as "being able to complete new matter forms, run conflict checks, open new matters, the intake process—it is much easier and quicker. I can do this from any location. I have noticed how it's like being in my old big firm, where I had all of this support that you typically don't have in a solo practice. This also includes invoicing and billing. All of this allows me to be more responsive to my clients. Many applications are free to use, or offered at a low cost. The time saved in the long run benefits efficiency. It can be challenging to create and organize all this on your own without the resources of a large law firm. Now you have access."

Nicole also uses Ruby Receptionists, a company that provides real, live reception services, but—and the caller would never know this—the receptionists are answering from an office in Portland, Oregon. Basically, Ruby Receptionists provides your law firm with the vocal services of an in-house receptionist, but at a fraction of the cost (you are not really employing a full-time person). Calls are transferred to you, as if they were originating from your lobby (but in the case of the VLOs, there isn't a lobby to begin with). Nicole loves how all of her calls are routed via the virtual reception service and are followed up with email messages. Another plus: Ruby Receptionists are known for their happy, friendly answering service, which is evidenced by their ranking in *Fortune* magazine as one of the Best Companies to Work for in Oregon. In the ever-increasing world of emails, texts, and robotic phone menus, this technology-meets-real-live-person approach marries the "efficient, cost-effective" aim with the always appreciated "meaningful connection" client service experience, leaving the law firm with a perfect recipe for success.

Nicole also uses mobile applications, which are computer programs designed specially to run on smartphones, tablets, and other mobile devices. In 2014, the Apple App Store and Google Play boast over 1.6 million apps, and that is just from two retailers. So, it is safe to say that apps are popular, and there are plenty to choose from. For law firms, there are thousands of apps that help with the practice of law and the marketing aspect of client development. Nicole particularly likes Dictate + Connect. This app allows Nicole the ability to dictate (like she would with a Dictaphone), and then the program creates an email message with the dictation attached to send to a colleague, assistant, or other contact. The app frees Nicole from tapes, computers, and cables, and the secure encryption adds to the app's usability.

Janet Ward Black

Partner, Ward Black Law

Tort Litigation

Janet Ward Black practices in Greensboro, North Carolina, where she is the principal owner of Ward Black Law. The 36-person firm is one of the largest woman-owned law firms in North Carolina, and they represent people primarily in personal injury, workers' compensation, and defective product actions. They also address family law and disability cases.

In Janet Ward's case, most people visiting her firm's website know about the firm's reputation, so they go to the site as the last endorsement before picking up the phone. As the firm saw increasing inquiries resulting from a "Contact Us" form on their site, they decided to try the live chat window. Janet Ward confirms that her firm has "found that the live chat feature has a really high success rate with people actually engaging" with the firm. Janet Ward continues, "People are becoming more comfortable with live chat, and for the type of work we do, a lot of people are making comparisons with other firms. So being responsive is crucial. Folks with a catastrophic injury may not be able to sleep at night and are able to interact with us at 2 a.m." With live chat windows, legal consumers are able to get information from a potential law firm at any hour, making the experience very customer service oriented.

Websites are part of our daily lives and, in our profession, serve as a communication tool as they tell a story, give information, and act as an introduction to our services and skills. One common complaint about websites is that they are a "one-way only" means of marketing. Some firms are curing that criticism by making their websites more interactive through live chat windows. These pop-up chat boxes are a way to immediately engage with potential clients, turning website traffic into instantaneous conversations.

Janet Ward's firm uses Cloud8Sixteen as their live chat window provider. It took approximately one year to set up the entire platform, and initially the firm had to work through the questions potential clients would be asked to gather the most useful information. Once configured, the questions were put into a form to be used by the chat window provider during the chat session. After a chat, the firm is sent an email almost immediately with all of the answers from the chat.

Then they can determine if the potential client is a good match for their firm, and if so, they are able to respond immediately, usually by phone or by email. With Cloud8Sixteen, Janet Ward's firm pays by the call, but not for existing clients or for matters that are unrealistic leads (for example, if the matter relates to a completely separate practice area that the firm does not handle). Janet Ward notes that live chat windows are ideal for practice areas including criminal, bankruptcy, and family law. This technology is particularly helpful for practice areas that normally get cold calls. At first blush, "I believe any practice area that is dealing with individuals can benefit."

Today, Janet Ward's firm is averaging 4,000 new client intakes per year. To track client intake, the firm uses a database that pulls together the data regarding intakes. Then monthly reports classify the source of new intakes. Additionally, the database captures and reports on why people contacted the firm, how they went about doing so, and if the firm took the case. The firm carefully tracks the details so that they can understand what is working, and then they focus their marketing on those successful approaches. Again, we see that well-researched, focused technology applications can save money and streamline processes to better support the business of law firms. Working smarter, not harder— that is what infusing technology into the practice of law is all about.

It is important to note that when designing and implementing a pop-up live chat window, you should make sure that the technology is fully mobile device friendly. In other words, the live chat window needs to fit a phone's small screen. And make sure the "close" function for the pop-up window is accessible. If web visitors are unable to access your site because the pop-up window is stuck on their device, you can be sure they will close your website and visit a competitor's.

Janet Ward also profiled two unique, helpful telephone technologies that are making a positive impact on her practice. First is the call-tracking service she uses to identify how calls originate. For example, her firm has specific call-tracking service numbers that are placed in various media sources. "When someone calls the firm on a specific number, we are able to ID and track where they are calling from. This allows us to decipher where our potential clients are finding out about us—from television to the web to billboards," explains Janet Ward. "We use New Call Solutions; it's an intake phone system that is very specialized in the legal industry," she continues. And, of course, when asked why this is so important, her response is not at all surprising: "We want to make sure we are making wise investments."

Secondly, Janet Ward shared that New Call Solutions also offers Intake Academy. This service allows for Janet Ward's staff to be trained on the technology being utilized in the office. "They listen to our staged calls and give us feedback," she shares. "We also track how many appointments are made as a result of the calls, and the quality of each call." Combining technology with training is the best way to ensure your investment is going to pay off. Finally, adding in good metrics and a tracking methodology is a superb plan to allow for tweaks and tune-ups to perfect your office tech.

Janet Ward also uses apps to enhance her practice, just like Nicole. Recently, Janet Ward's firm created a car wreck app that "allows people to take pictures, and to know what [to] do when accidents happen," she explains. "It gives us zing. We are using it to add value to our services, and also to remind people that we litigate personal injury cases, especially automobile accidents." Janet Ward continues, "It's a tool that shows we have something helpful, something cutting-edge, just for you."

Amy Angel
Partner, Barran Liebman LLP
Employment Law

Amy Angel practices in Portland, Oregon, where she represents public and private employers in all stages of employment litigation, including advice and compliance, administrative complaints, and trial as well as appeal. Amy works with employers of all sizes, from small local companies to national companies with operations in Oregon, and in a wide variety of industries, including construction, retail, manufacturing, agriculture, law, and health care, just to name a few. Amy is a big fan of her phone—the functions available and the mobility it gives her to respond to clients seamlessly. As commercials show us, and our daily use confirms, telephones have come a long way since Bell discovered how to transmit vocal sounds. Now, we can host hundreds on conference calls, leave voice mails, transfer calls, and enjoy a plethora of other telephone technologies that make communicating occur at a rapid pace. In a law firm, where time is money, telephones and all their accompanying bells and whistles can make a notable difference. The right telephone can be critical for the attorney who travels a great deal and refuses to compromise client service when out of the office.

Two tools that help Amy manage calls and stay connected via telephone with clients are the twinning feature and auto-email of voice mails from her desk phone. The mobile twinning technology allows an external phone line (like Amy's office land line) to ring through to her cell phone. With twinning, the ability to stay connected is impressively easy, and the days of missed calls and phone tag are over—benefiting Amy, her clients, and colleagues.

Another useful phone technology is voice mail to email. This feature immediately sends voice mails left on Amy's office land line to email, affording Amy easy access to pick up her voice mails from her iPhone, which is synched with her office email. If follow-up is needed by her assistant or another member of the firm, she simply forwards the email, and that recipient has the ability to play the voice mail from her own email. Staying connected and being responsive, especially when out of the office, is a signature of a dedicated professional—and phones these days give Amy the tools she need to make this happen.

Amy's firm also is a big proponent of Google Alerts, a program that monitors the Web for interesting new content at your direction. The simple tool is one of Amy's favorites, and rightly so. "I love being able to set alerts on different cutting-edge laws I am following, client names, and my target potentials. Once set, anything published on the Web dumps directly into my inbox," Amy explains. The free, very convenient tool is really a great way to stay on top of your game, from legal news to client or target information. As Amy puts it, "Being in-the-know is priceless. The whole concept is genius and it takes less than ten seconds to set up each alert." To set up alerts for yourself, just Google the words "Google Alerts" and you'll be walked through the "Create An Alert" process with ease.

Deborah Sperati

Partner, Poyner Spruill

Creditors' Rights, Financial Services, and Bankruptcy

Deborah Sperati, a partner at Poyner Spruill, works as a creditors' rights, financial services, and bankruptcy attorney. Much of her work has included lender liability defense, loan workouts, and loan restructures (commercial, initially). Deborah's firm has found extreme success with custom software, also known as bespoke software. This growing trend in law firms is known for meeting specific needs and attorney practice styles, which differ greatly across all practice areas, demographics, and personalities. Deborah explains that "with the real estate crisis, lenders needed foreclosure teams to handle foreclosures countrywide. During the boom, we were doing 1,000 foreclosures a month and there was a lot of pressure to do things faster, but it was very important to us to maintain the high quality of work."

So, what did Deborah and her firm do to get the work done *and* do it well? "In 2004, our internal IT team worked with our attorneys and dedicated and knowledgeable staff to develop e4Close, an automated workflow process for foreclosures specific to our state, which streamlined the entire process for us and our clients," Deborah answers. The program allows for document automation, structuring, and tracking foreclosures. It took Deborah's firm four months to develop the program, and after it was patented, they sold it to banks.

"The initial rollout was with existing clients," Deborah relays. Her firm made presentations and offered training to bank clients, both in person and via webinars using GoToMeeting software.

Deborah notes that the "most important thing was providing constant training and resources. For a firm our size (130 lawyers), this would be something that is indicative of the firm's commitment to the long run. There was a significant cost for our firm on the front end, but the payoff was big because it kept us in the forefront of the banking industry and in the running with the bigger firms. We wouldn't have been able to maintain 1,000 foreclosures a month without an automated system. It facilitated our ability to handle a large volume of cases, which paid off firm-wide when the recession impacted other areas of the firm."

Once Deborah's firm was successful in selling the software to clients, they moved to bigger markets and marketed e4Close by tabling at trade shows or other industry events and handing out demo DVDs to potential clients. "We showed how the product can be customized, in both the foreclosure and asset management arenas," explains Deborah. Quite impressive is this law firm of Deborah's—from seeing a need, to creating the technology in-house, to making the software into a sellable and profitable product. Now, these lawyers are businesspeople!

In addition to e4Close, Deborah also uses online portals, customized to her firm's needs by SharePoint. This technology is specific to client service and management. Clients are able to log in and review the case action log, which would equate to calling to get a case update.

> "No lawyer went to law school to be called a vendor, but it's required to keep clients."

Deborah explains that the client portal "is offered to clients who have 30-plus matters with the firm. This is more helpful for me as an attorney because it tracks what is being done, and it is so much easier than doing an attorney chronology eight months down the road. This is also really important for our clients. Clients have real-time access to their files. I think as banks become more regulated, it is crucial to have data available for their matters. They have vendor management groups that audit their law firms. We had to move to using technology."

Now Deborah knows that "no lawyer went to law school to be called a vendor, but it's required to keep clients." Deborah's firm demonstrates forward thinking and action, something all clients can appreciate. Additionally, Deborah shares, "It's great to have discussions with clients so you can see what they need. The conversations give me all this insight into where the client is going."

The software has also helped save business. Deborah explains, "Our largest client was a bank with whom we worked for many years, and then they were bought out by a much larger bank. We met with the new bank and showed them e4Close and our SharePoint client portal. I think having the technology and presenting it to them made a huge difference in our ability to keep them as clients."

Deborah's firm was able to demonstrate that they could handle the thousands of accounts, and that all of the information for each matter would be visible through the portal. "We got every bit of work we could have gotten because we had something to distinguish ourselves. Our pitch was, 'This is how we can make your lives easier,' and it worked," Deborah shares proudly—and deservedly so. Doesn't Deborah's story inspire you to start working on something customized tonight? Start making that wish list and remember, the up-front cost and time might be intimidating, but the benefits might just be worth it.

Conclusion

The goal of this chapter was to provide an overview of exceptional technologies that can enrich the practice of law and client development. From Rachel Rodgers's virtual law office, to client relationship management software and marketing videos, to Janet Ward Black's live chat window, telephone technologies, and car accident app, I hope you have been inspired to try tech tools in your office. There is no right or wrong way to use these products and practices; rather, it is all about becoming aware of the many tools available and choosing the best fit for your law firm. As the business of law continues to evolve through technology, my hope is that attorneys will see the options, the value, and the bright future of the products available for law office use.

Chapter 10

A Different Approach

Eleanor Southers

Doing things differently is sometimes seen as thinking in a unique way. We sometimes even say it is thinking and behavior that is "outside the box." So what does that mean? We all have ideas about what it might pertain to, but have you ever given it enough thought to decide if thinking differently, or outside the box, was worthwhile—and if so, exactly how to go about it?

We will look at four women who exemplify this thinking and find out how it has influenced and nurtured their marketing success. But first, just for the fun of it, let's see where the term *outside the box* came from and how it might apply to thinking differently.

Outside the box is a metaphor that means to think differently, unconventionally, or from a new perspective. That seems pretty simple, but when we look closely, we find that it is not such a simple thing to do. In fact, most people, when presented with a problem, definitely think inside the box. This means that they think within a structure and have a formula for attacking problems. Outside the box, on the other hand, requires lateral thinking.

There are three kinds of thinking: lateral, vertical logic, and horizontal imagination. Lateral thinking is solving the problems through an indirect and creative approach, using reasoning that is not immediately obvious. Vertical logic thinking is the traditional way of using the step-by-step approach with the given data. That is the way we were taught in law school. Last, horizontal imagination thinking creates lots of ideas but very little implementation.

Where did the term *thinking outside the box* come from? It seems that there were management consultants in the 1970s and 1980s who were challenged to solve a puzzle. Here is the puzzle:

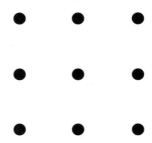

They were asked to connect the dots of the puzzle by using one line only and never lifting their pencil. As you can see, the dots form a "box." In order to solve the puzzle, the person had to use lateral thinking and go "outside the box," as shown here:

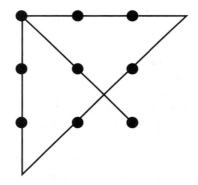

Thus, we have thinking outside the box.

The tester also found that they got the best results from the test takers, not by telling them to draw outside the box, but by speaking to the test takers in a nonjudgmental, free association style. That helped them to find solutions. This would seem to indicate that criticism hinders lateral thinking. Could that be why not much lateral thinking goes on in law school?

This is obviously why brainstorming works so well when a group sits down without critical input and develops ideas to solve a problem.

With the advent of Silicon Valley, working and solving problems with a team approach has reached new heights. Failure is now more acceptable and understood to go hand in hand with lateral thinking. Vertical thinking seems more secure, but in a competitive environment, the way to make rain and market more successfully is to definitely think differently and outside the box.

So let's see how these successful and courageous women have used their lateral thinking to increase their business and, I bet, have more fun while breaking traditional barriers.

You will be meeting four women who have made a variety of professional choices. Kathy Sherman is an associate at a midsized firm in San Jose, California (i.e., Silicon Valley). She started her law career later in life after gaining significant experience in other fields. Kathy sees this as a distinct advantage in getting to where she has in her career. You'll be excited to read her story.

Pam Simmons comes to her professional life from a slightly different angle. She, too, didn't get an early start in the law but has worked that to her advantage to rise to the level of a forensic expert. As a partner in a small firm in Capitola, California, she has gained nationwide distinction as the "go-to" person for advice and direction on mortgages. Pam has used the crisis in the real estate world to focus her talents in an area that is definitely outside the box. She now is going on to explore further areas where she might be of value by sifting out the latest scams in the business arena.

Next, we have Pauline Will, who is a founding partner in a midsized firm in Buffalo, New York. You will want to follow her success as she climbs the ladder of her chosen profession. Pauline is a woman who knew exactly what she wanted at each turn in her career and took every advantage to obtain it. With that kind of direction, she has gotten to the top with extraordinary speed. I look forward to sharing some of her ideas about flexibility in doing things differently to get what you want.

Last, we have the wonderful new dean of the University of Santa Clara, School of Law, Lisa Kloppenberg. It is especially rewarding to highlight a woman who had to think differently to position herself in the best way to give back to the legal community. In the male-dominated world of academia, she was challenged to make her rain by taking advantage of every opportunity that came her way, while creating those opportunities that were a little slow in showing up. Lisa has much to teach young lawyers about how to conduct themselves as "legal rebels" to meet their rainmaking goals.

Let's get started . . .

Kathleen Sherman

Associate, Berliner Cohen

IP Litigation, Complex Commercial Litigation, and Criminal Defense

Making Experience an Advantage

I first met Kathleen—or Kathy, as she likes to be called—at an ABA Women Rainmakers seminar that I gave at her firm. I noticed that she was very quick to grasp the niche marketing idea I was selling and had her own interesting input that she shared with the group. I decided she would be a perfect candidate to interview for approaching a legal career in a different way.

Kathy is a woman who found her way to the law later in life. Her working life has been an exercise in vision combined with practicality.

Kathy graduated college with a degree in mathematics and computer science. She then went on to various positions, including software project manager at Hewlett-Packard, where she managed ten software engineers in releasing four new software packages. As Kathy tells it, "I took time out for motherhood but continued developing my skills by writing a book titled *A Housekeeper Is Cheaper Than a Divorce: Why You **CAN** Afford to Hire Help and How to Get It*." The book led to speaking engagements on radio and TV as well as more articles.

Then she felt the draw of law school and in 2005 graduated summa cum laude from Santa Clara University School of Law. While in law school, she took advantage of opportunities offered through the school's clinical experiences programs, including in Juvenile Dependency Court, the district attorney's office, a criminal defense firm, and the law school's community law center. Kathy emphasized that "acquiring courtroom experience as a bar-certified law clerk helped me brand myself as a valuable asset to potential employers."

The Juvenile Dependency externship came after visiting a criminal trial and talking to a young prosecutor who was also observing the trial. That discussion led her indirectly to Judge Leonard Edwards, the Juvenile Dependency Court supervising judge, who invited her to extern with him. Kathy's relationship with Judge Edwards was a valuable one, which helped her land subsequent internships and jobs. "If you don't ask, you don't get" is definitely the advice here.

After graduation, she worked for a short time as a contract attorney at the criminal defense firm where she had interned. She then went on to become a research attorney at the San Mateo County Superior Court, where she worked researching, advising, and writing extensively for the court in both civil and criminal cases.

Kathy explains that all this great experience led her to seek out a litigation position at a firm. Kathy saw this as a grand adventure because she was an older attorney competing with a distinctly younger Silicon Valley crowd. "I saw my age as an advantage, rather than a detriment. I believed that firms would see that I would be immediately 'client safe,' and I felt that my pre–law school experiences and greater maturity were strengths." Kathy approached her job search task with the same enthusiasm that she had demonstrated in the past. She told me that she identified and sent her resume to more than 200 desirable firms, some of which had posted job listings and some of which she contacted cold.

To accompany her resume, Kathy wrote a bang-up cover letter that the partner who hired her said was the best he had ever seen. Kathy did this by highlighting her strengths and what she could contribute to the firm. She said she "pointed out that my years of solid technical work coupled with my demonstrated ability to make persuasive arguments as a writer" would be of benefit to the firm. Mention of the internships and clerkships was extremely important in demonstrating how focused Kathy was in law school, as was a reference to her courtroom experience.

So began her journey at Berliner Cohen in San Jose, California, in 2009. Kathy chose this firm "because of the possibility of growth in a midsize environment with dynamic leadership." Entering as an associate, she immediately began thinking about rainmaking. Kathy "asked partners how to build a foundation for bringing business into the firm." Their response was to facilitate seminars.

The question, then, was what kind of seminars and in what venue. Knowing that her change of career late in life gave her a unique perspective, Kathy reached out to women's professional organizations and delivered a number of seminars. Subsequently, she was invited to be a guest on a television talk show sponsored by the American Association of University Women on the topic "Changing Careers after Forty." After obtaining a copy of the program on DVD, she uploaded it to YouTube and linked to the video from her law firm bio page and her LinkedIn profile.

By this time, she was practicing general business litigation and white-collar criminal defense. That is when she reports that she saw "a great opportunity to use my technology background to really start increasing my visibility in the firm." As one of the few attorneys in the firm with a technical background, Kathy was invited to staff a very complex technical case for a business client. After a successful resolution and finding that she "loved working on it," she saw an opportunity to expand her base within the firm.

First, Kathy took and passed the Patent Bar exam, qualifying her to practice before the U.S. Patent and Trademark Office and demonstrating her knowledge of patent law. Then she began to educate the partners about her newly established expertise and her interest in handling complex technical matters, letting them know that she could handle cases that might have been previously referred out. As a result, she was assigned several high-tech cases.

Then she worked on improving her online brand, emphasizing her high-tech expertise, on her firm's website and on social media. Because of this and her networking efforts, Kathy began to bring her own clients into the firm.

Next she intends to create seminars for high-tech clients. Kathy "plans to target newer, small to midsized tech firms that haven't yet gotten scooped up by the bigger firms." Kathy will focus on preventive measures that will help these potential new clients to protect their intellectual property. In-house counsel who might be able to use the firm's tech services is another niche that she will explore.

While Kathy will continue to practice general business litigation and white-collar criminal defense, she "will concentrate on better articulating that my focus is now on intellectual property." She plans to continue growing her practice, for her own and her firm's benefit, by bringing solid performance to an area that is a growth opportunity for her firm.

So what advice does Kathy have for her women rainmakers? First, they should "think about their personal and professional strengths, not just by themselves but by asking colleagues, friends, and family for input." Then, "look at how they are presenting themselves, online and in any printed materials. Do they sound like everyone else? How could their presentation be made distinctive? What strengths could be identified or emphasized? They should also consider what they have done that presents unique value to a client. How can that be conveyed? Are they team players? What leadership have they shown? Can they show that they can relate to a diversity of clients? What is their community involvement?"

When asked about how much of her time she spends marketing and networking, Kathy estimates, "I think I spend about 10 percent of my time on business development." She does point out that billable hours are important, but time for business development can be found by "staying focused at work." Very important to her is to put rainmaking events and opportunities on her calendar and then to just "do them." The opportunities have come her way by following a strict routine and combining her management skills with effective communication. In this way, she can pinpoint what she needs to get to the next step and get the support to do just that.

Kathy also continues to be involved in educational programs for women because it "allows her to meet high achievers who are leading women in technology in her community," going on to explain that "an exchange of knowledge and experience is the key to forming relationships that can create rainmaking experiences." And who knows what will come of that?

Pamela Simmons
Partner, Simmons and Purdy
Real Estate Law, Mortgage Lending

Niching Has Her Doing It Differently

Pam's story is like a trip down a serendipitous road. She tells me that she thinks of herself as "very flexible and simply looking at what is being presented to her and going with the flow." Considering all that she has accomplished, I would have to say that there is much more to it than that!

After raising her children ("children come first") and with a background in math, Pam decided to go to law school in the early '90s. She began her studies at a private law school that offered night classes but had a great opportunity to go to Tulane Law School in Paris, France, where she studied European law and mass tort litigation. Returning to her law school in California, she finished her studies and became a lawyer in 1992.

Probably the first karmic event was that Bill Purdy, her present partner, taught a class in tax law at her law school. Pam became Bill's law clerk at his firm during her last year and went on to an associate position with the law firm after graduation.

She worked on what was the largest fraud case in California while in law school. She also had the opportunity to be trained as a forensic accountant while working on that case. "I was so impressed with all the intricacies of this fraud case." Taking this fascination into the practice and expanding that into security fraud and white collar crime led her to a position with the Santa Cruz County District Attorney's Office. Here she had a chance to use her training as a forensic accountant when she was confronted with the overwhelming amount of paperwork in prosecuting an embezzlement matter.

"One of the strongest skills I developed at the DA's office was to make complex things understandable." This helped win cases and drew an offer from a close friend who had a small firm to join him. "Unfortunately, that didn't work out," and Pam formed her own solo firm on the spur of the moment.

Luckily, a client appeared who was being sued over a real estate deal, but then Pam had to find an office. Pam "rented a little office" but was faced with the prospect of needing about $20,000 to start the business.

"I boiled it down to $2,000 and started. Other attorneys in the suite helped me, and clients seemed to just come out of nowhere. I took anything I thought I could manage." As the firm grew, Pam longed to create a more upscale practice. She spoke to a mentor from her law clerk days who understood finance and her need for "bigger digs."

Then came the next chance happening in her life. "A tax attorney needed to close his solo firm and gave me his practice. I didn't know anything about tax and called Bill, who had just left his job due to the long commute! He came to see me on Monday morning, and two years later, after working together, we decided we were compatible and he became my partner."

As more and more tax work came in, which Bill handled, Pam decided she finally had to take some action of her very own. So here comes doing it differently: Pam hit on niching the consumer fraud practice, which she enjoyed, into mortgage fraud as it was raising its ugly head in the 2000s. She also continued to "carve out a niche handling more complex mortgage cases at the state federal and bankruptcy courts." Pam began doing truth in lending cases (TILA) in federal and state courts. She found it necessary to teach judges about the law regarding frauds being perpetrated by the lending institutions. Additionally, she took a case of 100 fraud victims because she could see the mortgage crisis coming.

Just when the practice was starting to really boom in 2007, Pam was diagnosed with a brain aneurism, which resulted in her being in a coma for a month. She had to take a substantial amount of time to learn to walk and function all over again. She was gone from the practice for many months but, fortunately, Bill carried the torch. In fact, Bill had become so fascinated by the mortgage fraud occurring that he had been learning that area of Pam's practice for a few years. He was able to step up and cover for her while she was recovering. Another kismet moment.

Surviving and coming back to practice, Pam knew that she needed to again go outside her normal range of doing business and create the type of practice that she could now handle that was more focused and less stressful. Targeting her overall goal of "helping consumers," she closed her litigation practice, settled cases to gain back some of the funds lost in her absence, and did a lot of TILA cases.

"Scammers were coming across all lines into the legal field. I was trying to help consumers with understanding that they did not need to pay big funds to attorneys for loan modifications." She assisted when she could in negotiating to keep them in their homes. So she now turned to more teaching and educating in consumer fraud. This meant she had to tackle sorting out the cases where she could help from those that were not doable.

Pam came up with the solution by crafting a method of hiring a contract attorney to conduct a telephone interview off-site and decide the cases where Pam could give advice as the first step. This decreased expenses and resulted in excellent service to her clients. She went on to develop a consultation format where she could explain all the options available to the homeowner, including the complex tax issues. Her past experience allowed her to again use her ability to make the complex understandable.

"I now have done thousands of these consultations, during which, for one hour of my time, the client gets all my years of expertise advising them of their choices and consequences. They walk away knowing all of their alternatives and can act as they see fit."

I asked her to name one of her favorite books. "I like *Who Moved My Cheese.*" I think this is because her cheese got moved a lot. As far as advice for rainmaking, Pam believes "being very flexible is important," and this also involves keeping up her own knowledge as the laws change.

Teaching has become very important as she strives to brand herself as an authority. Because the mortgage fraud area was such a hot topic by 2008, Pam's niche has worked out well. She has been interviewed on many shows and television programs explaining what is happening and advising people nationwide on the consequences of this economic crisis. This means that she and Bill travel extensively.

Additionally, it has been important for her to continue to produce articles on the subject of consumer protection, and she has contributed to the *CEB Practice Guide to Mortgages, Deeds of Trust and Foreclosures*. Pam explains that she sees her focus now to be on "information and teaching." She has done this by appearing at symposiums produced by the ABA Section of Real Property, Trust and Estate Law for several years. She is also an active member in and has spoken at the conferences of the National Association of Consumer Advocates. Pam "likes to teach real estate attorneys how to counsel their clients in protecting them from predators." She envisions free courses for real estate attorneys to alert them to future dangers as mortgage lending "is coming back to life."

But, always aware that she has to sell herself as an expert, she continues to present herself to newspapers and the media as the go-to person for insight into these real estate financial disasters that are always looming. She would like to take her expertise to public television to extend her audience in this very important work.

Pam tells us that she sees her future work, in addition to speaking and writing, as "constantly seeking to find the errors and mistakes in the financial world that I can identify and warn people about."

So, Pam's advice to women rainmakers involves being sure to "track referrals and reward them properly." She also wants women to reach out to more organizations and newspapers to get their stories out.

Although Pam did not put it in so many words, I came away having witnessed a woman with the amazing ability to take what comes her way but to also make it her own and build on it. Leveraging her abilities to produce an ongoing practice including forensic work while giving great service to her clients is a remarkable ability.

Pauline Will

Founding Partner, Bennett, Schechter, Arcuri & Will, LLP

Toxic Tort Litigation, Trucking and Transportation Law, Product Liability, Insurance Defense Litigation, Insurance Coverage Law

Focus, Flexibility, and Sacrifice Are Her Keys to Success

From the outside, it would appear that Pauline floated through her profession to become a partner early in her career while also creating a full personal life filled with a family and children. The truth is quite different. This young woman has had the foresight and vision to accomplish clear, concise goals that through hard work and focus have established an amazing career early in her life.

Pauline's story starts with interning as a student law clerk for a Federal District Court judge in law school and then moving into the district attorney's office after graduation as a prosecutor. Pauline recalls, "I was getting a lot of trial experience but really wanted to exclusively handle felony trials." After two years, when that was not forthcoming, she took some time to have her first baby. "I was back at work when a colleague called me and told me about a firm that was hiring a litigation associate that may be a good fit for me."

Acting on the advice, Pauline contacted the firm even though she had just had a baby. "I told the firm I was looking for part-time litigation work, and they hired me." A big part of her consideration was that she wanted to stay involved in litigation and not be out of the loop for too much time.

So in 2002, Pauline started her journey with a private law firm. She added another baby to her family but was able to keep up her involvement, if only part time (as we in law know, this is full time anywhere else). Pauline mentions that this is because she "worked very hard and was quite flexible." She established a good relationship with the firm's partners, who saw her bringing value to the firm as a whole.

Now Pauline had to decide how to do this differently by not falling back on many women's practice of just waiting for promotion to be offered. Instead, as Pauline describes it, "In taking both the firm and my needs into consideration, I demonstrated that I was capable of providing for the firm's needs while still having a flexible schedule."

Pauline's recollection of helping her father, who was a small business owner, provided her with the experience and insight into how to do this. By observing how important business development was to the business, "I was able to make a thoughtful decision that to continue working hard on the partners' cases was in the best interest of the firm." Along with this came the insight that she "found it liberating to have a client with a legal issue that I could handle."

Soon, she wanted to have cases of her own. This meant bringing in several personal injury clients. More importantly, this grew into expanding existing clients with the partners' blessing. "I started handling toxic tort and lead paint defense as niches for the firm's existing clients, and the partners were very generous in their acknowledgment of my contribution." Here again, we see thinking in selecting niches that are not only relevant but can produce results.

This led Pauline to determine that she would like to be an equity partner in the firm. But this also meant personal and financial sacrifice and required Pauline to step back from her original path. This worked, and she became an equity partner in 2008—a remarkable feat for someone so young.

Pauline attributes most of her success to carefully building relationships with insurance carriers and self-insurers. She insists that "listening to their needs is the most important element of relationship building." Of course, she also had to articulate exactly what she does and how she could help them.

Much of this ability to make rain also comes from the fact that she was handling litigation in a male-dominated trucking industry. This allows her to distinguish herself as a major player and a very competent woman. The addition of the niches in toxic torts and lead paint defense has increased her visibility and supported her growth.

One of the most exciting events happened recently, when several of the partners of her firm broke away to start their own firm. Pauline was one of them and has been a pivotal force in establishing a new, powerful firm willing to really meet the needs of their clients, thus demonstrating that outside-the-box thinkers need to take risks.

As far as advice to women attorneys, Pauline has several thoughts: "Get the partners involved in your growth," "Work hard and be true to yourself," and "Be willing to take risks and realize that you may have to make difficult choices and sacrifices along the way."

Always looking to find the next level at the firm is also important. This may be with the help of a mentor or sponsor in a large firm. Pauline took a slightly different path and went outside the box by finding a business coach through the women's business center sponsored by her alma mater. There, she also found the support and advice she needed to advance at a fast pace and the business model to keep following in her father's footsteps.

Pauline estimates, "I spend at least a half a day a month planning my marketing." This is, of course, on top of taking every opportunity to build further business relationships for the firm. All of this hard work and flexibility has produced optimum results and personal satisfaction with the practice of law.

Lisa Kloppenberg
Dean, Santa Clara University, School of Law

Constitutional Law and Appropriate Dispute Resolution

Doing It Differently in Academia
Although this book is about women rainmakers, I wanted to include a woman in academia who has shown a lot of outside-the-box thinking in scaling the ivy-covered walls. Much can be learned from a woman who has chosen this path within the law using the same kind of focus that is needed to make traditional rain. The end product may be different, but it takes planning and effort similar to that required in creating a profitable career in a firm or as a solo. Lisa credits much of her early success to the dean of her law school, Dorothy Nelson. Ms. Nelson has gone on to become a judge on the Ninth Circuit Court of Appeals, and Lisa says "she was a great role model and mentor." Judge Nelson has come back occasionally to the University of Southern California to teach a course and is still a great resource for this dean.

This relationship led Lisa to clerk for Judge Nelson after law school, which strengthened the bond that supports her even today.

On the heels of her clerkship, Lisa moved to Washington, DC, and took a job at Kaye, Scholer, Feirman, Hays and Handler. It was here she met Ken Fineberg, who "introduced me to ADR [alternative dispute resolution] and mediation." Mr. Fineberg went on to become a giant in the area of catastrophic events payout funds administration. As an appointed special master, he gave his time on a pro bono basis to determine compensation and distribute awards for the 9/11 fund. Additionally, he oversaw the BP spill fund and has gone on to such other funds as the Sandy Hook, Aurora, and Boston Marathon funds. Mostly, this has been done on a pro bono basis.

"Ken gave me a well-rounded education," Lisa says, and she went on to include these ADR skills and newly learned negotiation techniques both in her life and in the curriculums of the schools where she taught.

With a husband in law school, next came babies, and with that came a "search for balance." "I had a seed planted at USC that I could teach," Lisa explains. "So, I went to what is called the 'Meat Market' in DC, where all the interviews took place for academia." Lisa landed in Oregon, at University of Oregon School of Law, where she stayed for ten years, receiving tenure.

At Oregon, Lisa taught her favorite mediation courses and "promoted experiential learning." Every student was encouraged to do an externship and develop skills that would help them in the workplace.

In 2001, her book titled *Playing It Safe: How the Supreme Court Sidesteps Hard Cases and Stunts the Development of Law* was published. She coauthored another publication, *Resolving Disputes: Theory, Practice and Law*, which was a little less confrontational for the conservative world.

> *"Be willing to take risks and realize that you may have to make difficult choices and sacrifice along the way."*

Judge Nelson gave Lisa a call and "recommended me for a deanship." This came with a move to Dayton, Ohio, and to the law school at the University of Dayton. There, she was the university's first female dean and worked to create a higher profile for the law school. "I also started a lawyer-as-problem-solver program and created a nationally recognized two-year accelerated degree option, which is a good option for some lawyers."

Then came the opportunity to move back to California, where she and her husband have family. A Jesuit institution, Santa Clara University School of Law, offered her the position of dean, which she started in July 2013. Having been in the legal world as a private lawyer made Lisa well aware of the need to better prepare students to get work after law school. She is a part of the California State Bar Task Force on Admissions, which is revamping California law schools' requirements to include 15 hours of practical learning, 50 hours of pro bono work, and ten units of MCLE in addition to the regular curriculum. She is a very valuable member of this task force because of her private practice background as well as all the career development innovations that she has already implemented at her previous law schools.

It was important for her to involve the alumni in working with students on their future careers. "I also have a strong interest in preparedness for practice to be taught by the faculty," she explains. "Practical programs built onto social justice programs need to be in place to complement each other."

The Jesuit foundational values of head, hands, and heart are integrated into the curriculum, so there is a strong foundation for a complete education. Nestled in the Silicon Valley, the School of Law has vast resources that the dean expects to tap.

So let's get to the good part. Lisa had a lot of advice for women lawyers and rainmakers. "I couldn't have done what I have without the support of men. My husband has been incredibly helpful as well as encouraging to me in my career." Lisa says that women "should just make it happen." She is big believer in networking and building relationships. Her advice is to volunteer for organizations and nurture relationships with family and law school friends.

She recalls a female faculty member in Oregon who told Lisa that she shouldn't have tried to obtain tenure while having children. The dean feels we have to "break down these ideas." We should be also questioning judicial doctrine. In other words, "be a rebel," she says. "Going against conventional wisdom" is another favorite idea of the dean's. Her life and work have proven that she has done just that.

I asked her about her rainmaking skills in fundraising, which is such an important aspect of her job and very much the same experience as for women lawyers in practice (getting people to support your cause, be it getting more clients or more donors). Here Lisa adds that "fundraising is about relationship building and matchmaking. This means finding connections between donors' passions and the strengths of a law school or organization." She goes on to add, "I think many stereotypically female qualities (e.g., listening, empathy, emotional intelligence) are helpful in building relationships and matching the hopes and dreams of supporters to particular visions and projects."

It's easy to see that Lisa has had to constantly come up with creative ideas, not only to fundraise but to keep inspiring faculty and students to aim for new, exciting activities that will in turn benefit the law school. While keeping many balls in the air, Lisa has and will continue to reinvent the way that women in academia will be viewed. This is certainly leadership at its highest level, and the benefit will be felt by women lawyers for years to come.

Conclusion

So what does this all mean for the women lawyers trying to think differently in their own professional lives? These examples have several elements in common. None of these women left her family life out of her plans. Each was able to establish a satisfactory arrangement so that she could benefit from her decisions and sacrifices.

These women also took chances. Kathy didn't let the fact that she was a mature woman slow her down in cementing lofty goals for herself. She worked hard, as did all the women, in making sure that she would be known for her devotion to the tasks at hand. So perhaps that is the first lesson here: that hard work is an important foundation to build a profession on.

Secondly, as described above, calculated risk is also necessary to not just go along with the other sheep. This means that careful planning is the step that needs to be taken before anything else gets accomplished.

Being flexible also seems to be very important: grabbing opportunities as they present themselves and also saying "no" when appropriate. Basically, it comes down to really letting yourself think thoughts that are unlike those of many people around you. Creating your career is definitely thinking outside the box and it takes grit and tenacity to obtain results. But as you can see, it's well worth it!

Chapter 11

Final Thoughts: Get Retained

Beth Marie Cuzzone

You have read success story after success story in the preceding chapters about how women rainmakers use marketing techniques and tools to reach their professional goals. Marketing is the range of activities, including blogging, attending events, speaking, writing articles, and creating Web content as well as actively networking, that make you well known among potential clients. It's important to note that marketing lays the groundwork for building a practice, but your sales techniques will close business and bring clients in the door.

Sales techniques are the one-to-one activities you engage in based on a person's or company's particular legal needs.

Marketing activities are one-to-many efforts:
- Speeches
- Article writing
- Blog posts
- Television appearances

Sales activities are one-to-one actions:
- Meetings
- Strategy sessions
- Solving a particular problem

Marketing: one to many

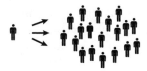

Sales: one to one

The Buying Cycle

The progression of converting a prospect to your client is a process. We will review this process, also known as the buying cycle, from the eyes of your client.

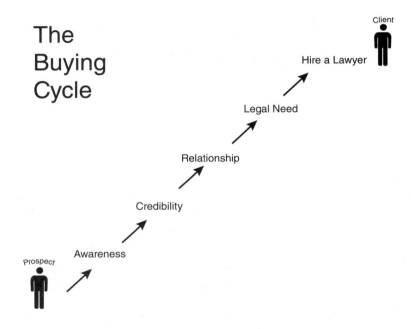

Awareness

Awareness is the first stage of the process for your prospective buyer. In chapter 7, we discussed developing your image or brand. What do you want to be known for? Divorce, international M&A, estate planning, litigation, workman's compensation, or something else? It's also important to be clear about what you do and whom you can help. The answers to these simple questions will drive the development of and your success with the awareness stage with prospects. In chapter 7, we discussed identifying *your* personal brand, and Katy Goshtasbi shared the following three-part definition of personal branding:

1. Identify the essence of your relevant attributes—that is, document your uniqueness.
2. Consistently communicate the essence of your relevant attributes to your audience (i.e., target market or prospects).

3. Learn and interpret how the audience perceives your brand message.

Each woman in chapter 7 chose to narrow and focus her brand instead of trying to be all things to all people. An even more important commonality among the interviewees is the existence of sincerity. In each instance, the women have stayed true to themselves, and instead of apologizing for being a woman, single mother, or wife, they have embraced those traits and incorporated them into their personal brand.

Karimah Lamar, from chapter 7, knows her uniqueness and utilizes her story well. She captures her target market's attention when networking or meeting with potential clients by making sure that "they connect with my story, the collection of experiences that define who I am. Sharing that story is very intentional and allows me to cultivate relationships in a more intimate way. It is not just about selling my services, but building long-lasting relationships," says Karimah.

Your website image, written brochures, external messaging, and advertising will help buyers learn about what you do and whom you help. Creating awareness means your name has familiarity to potential referral sources and clients. In chapter 4, Esther Lim discusses the types of activities she engages in to create awareness among her peers and target market, including editing a newsletter, presenting at seminars, visiting associations and governmental agencies, and working as a university professor. As Esther becomes top of mind, she is also adding credibility to her brand, which is the next step in the process.

Credibility

After the awareness stage, the small process ladder moves to the second phase, credibility. During this phase of the buying cycle, your target market forms an opinion of you. Being known and being credible in the marketplace are very different. Being a smart, savvy lawyer who knows the law is not enough to compete in today's marketplace; creating credibility is critical to the process.

To be credible, you must communicate to potential clients that you are not only good at solving legal problems, but someone who can obtain results. In several chapters, we read about marketing tools and

techniques that helped women rainmakers establish a desirable reputation. Writing and publishing content is a strong avenue to pursue.
Where to place your content is critical. Be sure to understand where
your target market turns for news and information so you may place
your content within those mediums.

In chapter 3, we read about the phenomena of social media. Social
media can act as a springboard to help you distribute your content to
many. LinkedIn, Facebook, Twitter, blogs, Pinterest, Google+, and
YouTube are just the start of technology platforms to come. Several
of the rainmakers in chapter 3 shared examples that illustrate ways
content and creditability help get you hired.

Ruth Carter, in chapter 3, gets emails at least once a week from
people who say, "I saw your blog about X. Can I talk to you about
my problem?" In the same chapter, Catherine Tucker, who focuses
on reproductive law, has found a way beyond speaking and writing to
communicate to potential clients by using visual posts. Her Pinterest
page communicates empathy and education along with a command
of the legal issues. These are both examples of matching your content
to your target market.

Relationship

Once you have established awareness and credibility in the market,
your buyer is more apt to cultivate a relationship with you. The relationship phase is usually the longest phase of the buying cycle. Consider these statistics: the legal industry states that it takes an average
of six to eight "touches" before you are hired. Another way to think
of it: from relationship to getting hired is an average of 18 months to
36 months.

First, you must "meet your market." By now, you have identified
the types of people and companies you want to represent and have
been working on delivering them content—speeches, articles, newsletters, blogs, tweets. It's time to reach out to people—either meeting
new prospects or reengaging with existing ones. Target markets are
usually defined by a geography, demographic, industry, or legal need.
So, be sure to find groups of people with the types of legal needs you
provide. Industry groups, trade associations, and affinity groups are a
good place to start. Here are a few examples:

Table 11.1. Ways to Meet Your Target Market

Examples of Target Markets (Potential Clients or Referral Sources)	Groups or Associations to Join
In-house counsel	Association of Corporate Counsel (need a referral)
Construction industry	Association of Building Contractors
Other lawyers	Bar associations
Custody/divorce	Associations of mediators and family counseling
Residential real estate	Local broker association
Chief financial officers	CFO organizations
Hospitals/universities	University nonprofit associations

The possibilities are endless. Once you join an association, the key to success will be to become involved in the association. You may volunteer on committees, membership drives, fundraising, or event organization. Your involvement will provide you the opportunity to build relationships with the people who have problems you can solve or needs you can meet.

In chapter 7, Karimah Lamar acknowledges, "Prior to having a defined brand, I was not building quality relationships. I would attend different events, meet people, and rarely connect again. After I began to consciously think about my brand and develop it, my marketing efforts became more focused and purposeful. I had a defined plan that allowed me to meet people, engage them, and actually create meaningful relationships."

Let's look at where we are in the process. Now your prospect knows what you do, believes you are good at it, and knows who you are. It's time to keep your relationship alive and top of mind. Consider how long you have known someone before you have a need to hire them. Just because you know someone, it doesn't mean you will retain them, correct? The same principle applies to you. Just because someone knows you doesn't mean they will hire you. Keeping in touch and staying top of mind is a difficult task. In chapter 3, we read about the use of social media to help you establish credibility. Social media will also significantly help you maintain relationships with prospects when there are no active legal problems to solve.

This book is chock-full of ideas to illustrate how women rainmakers have turned articles and speeches (credibility building) into relationship building by adapting an article, blog, or speech specific to a particular company or person.

Now the process has moved from marketing (one to many) into sales (one to one). In our communication chapter (chapter 4), woman rainmaker Grace Parke Fremlin puts it best: "You must keep the relationship fresh and current. You must visit, have meetings, phone calls, emails, lunches, and dinners. These should be as frequent as possible." Over time, your relationship will grow as well as the possibility of working together.

Legal Need

There is a natural progression from relationship to legal need. Some people use the term *lead nurturing*. You have been building rapport and trust with prospects. And you have been helping them stay informed about a legal issue that is important to them. Some lawyers wait for the legal need, and some lawyers create the need, or "trigger," to get hired. An example of waiting for a legal need may be when a litigation defense lawyer positions herself as the go-to lawyer once someone is sued. She doesn't have any control over when a prospect has a claim filed or when she will be hired. It's a wait-and-see process. On the other hand, an example of creating a need, or "trigger," is when an employment lawyer offers to conduct an assessment of a company's employment risk and suggests ways to reduce the risk by training, drafting handbooks, and helping the company create an offensive strategy—thereby creating a need, or "trigger," to be hired.

Buyers also use all types of criteria when choosing counsel. Some people hire a lawyer based on her "win rate" or success ratio, some hire a lawyer based on her "deal personality," others will hire a lawyer based on the name and reputation of the law firm, and so on. Your responsibility during the relationship stage is to understand the criteria that are important to the person who will hire you and to know when he or she will have legal needs you may solve.

The more questions you ask, the more opportunity you will have to present solutions to your prospect. As Grace Parke Fremlin states earlier in the book, "You must be in touch with the decision maker or someone who can get you to that person. Cold calling does not work. . . . When the client brings a need or demand to you, you must match the reputation of the firm and then look to see what relevant work you can do for the client."

Hiring a Lawyer

At this point in the relationship, you have done the following:

- Targeted and communicated (awareness)
- Increased your visibility and credibility (credibility)
- Built rapport with members of your target market (relationship)
- Identified their legal needs and developed potential solutions (legal need)

Now, finally, it is time to ask for the business and obtain the client. Asking for business can be the most difficult and uncomfortable part of the process. In fact, most lawyers can get comfortable with every stage of the process except this one—asking for business and getting hired. Asking for business doesn't have to be as painful as you might expect. If you can shift your mindset from "selling something" to "offering a solution to someone's problem," a lot of the discomfort will be alleviated. You have asked good questions and listened carefully in the relationship and legal need stages. Therefore, you are offering a solution—you are not just asking someone to hire you.

A problem that is seen all too often is when lawyers want to move from introductions to getting hired in the same meeting. It doesn't happen frequently—unless your prospect has received your name from someone he or she trusts and respects *and* has a burning problem that your skill set can immediately resolve. In this instance, the whole buying process can happen in one meeting. Don't doubt the value of building trust and a solid relationship. It takes time and patience.

There is no off-the-shelf script to ask for business—one size does not fit all—and it will likely be different each and every time you ask. Below are a few generic ways of asking:

- "I'd like the opportunity to help you resolve this issue."
- "Would you like me to review the contract off the clock and give you my thoughts on negotiating the terms?"
- "May we work together on your next matter?"
- "Do you have an 'approved' list of lawyers who are prevetted by your company? How may I be considered to be placed on that list?"

If the answer to any of these is "no," try to understand the reasons for not getting hired. Understanding the reason(s) will give you an opportunity to clarify any misperceptions your prospect may have about you and/or your firm. Overcoming objections is one of the most common stumbling blocks when trying to convert a prospect to a client. Have you ever heard any of the following comments?

- "My board of directors doesn't know your firm's reputation."
- "We are looking for a firm with a national platform."
- "We are only moving forward with firms that can offer us alternative fee arrangements."
- "We don't like to use large firms."
- "We only hire small firms for this work."
- "Your hourly rates are higher than those of any other firm I use."
- "We use Johnson & Kenna as our law firm for most of our deals."

These objections should be the beginning of a dialog, not the end of the conversation. "Your hourly rates are higher than those of any other firm I use" is a perfect time to discuss budget, efficiency, and overall cost. Or, "My board of directors doesn't know your firm's reputation" is an opportunity to offer to provide more information about your firm to the prospect's board of directors.

No matter the situation, don't take it personally. Remember, people hire lawyers for all different types of reasons. If there is an instance that you aren't the right fit, please continue to build the relationship and wait for the next situation to offer a solution.

The second greatest mistake lawyers make is falling out of touch with a contact in their target market after the first "no" (the first greatest mistake is failing to ever ask for business).

Although it sounds counterintuitive, lost business is seldom truly lost. There is a strong likelihood you may still represent your prospect in the future if you focus on the relationship, not just getting hired for one specific instance. Consider what happens if your prospect's lawyer experiences any of the following:

- Has a conflict on a certain matter
- Transitions to an in-house position
- Doesn't communicate well or provide the results expected

Those situations are common, and there's a good possibility they will call upon you, if you've continued your connection.

So, remember, if the client says no, be resilient and keep in touch. Your objective is to help people with problems or opportunities, so don't shy away from "the ask"—and get retained.

Index